ROCK
GARDENING

ROCK GARDENING

Will Ingwersen

WARD LOCK LIMITED · LONDON

ACKNOWLEDGEMENTS

The publishers gratefully acknowledge the following agencies for granting permission to reproduce the following colour photographs: the Harry Smith Horticultural Photographic Collection (Front cover and Plates 1, 6, & 20); Pat Brindley (Plates 3, 13 & 16); and Michael Warren (Plates 10 & 14). The remaining colour photographs were taken by Robin Fletcher and are copyright Ward Lock Limited.

All the line drawings are by Wendy Bramall.

© Ward Lock Limited 1989

First edition, © Ward Lock, by Will Ingwersen published 1982

Second edition, first published in Great Britain in 1989
by Ward Lock Limited, 8 Clifford Street,
London W1X 1RB, an Egmont Company.

House editor Denis Ingram

Text filmset in Bembo
by Hourds Typographica, Stafford

Printed and bound in Portugal by Resopal

British Library Cataloguing in Publication Data

Ingwersen, Will
   Rock gardening. — Second ed.
     1. Gardens. Rock plants: Alpine plants — Encyclopaedias
   1. Title
   635.9'672

ISBN 0-7063-6742-1

CONTENTS

Preface 6

1   What alpine plants are and their basic needs 7
     Constructing a rock garden – Peat beds and walls – The alpine house

2   Propagation 13
     Seeds – Cuttings – Division

3   An alphabetical list of desirable alpine plants 17

4   Plants for special positions and conditions 88

     Index 93

PREFACE

This is not a book offered to the already expert grower of alpine plants, but is written for those not-too-knowledgeable amateur gardeners who are discovering an interest in, and love for, alpine plants. For such as these the standard text books may prove more discouraging than encouraging. It is my desire that the beginner should discover in these pages helpful information which is sufficiently detailed without being heavily technical and which will animate a developing interest.

What the book will provide in simple terms are the basic principles of alpine gardening and how to go about growing these jewels of the plant world, with or without the aid of a conventional rock garden. Information will be found on such matters as the construction of a rock garden and the various alternative methods of growing them which will provide a maximum of success and pleasure.

Inevitably, with increasing knowledge and skill, comes the desire to propagate one's own plants, and the basic methods of increase are outlined. The largest section of the book is devoted to an alphabetically arranged list of desirable plants. Obviously it cannot be comprehensive, for there are many thousands from which to choose, but it will enable you to form a nucleus collection which can be expanded as interest and knowledge increases.

As an additional aid to selection there are lists on the final pages of plants for specific places and purposes.

Whether your garden is large or small, there is a place in it for alpine plants and it is my hope that this small book may set your feet upon a path leading to an immensely satisfying and rewarding pastime.

W.I.

CHAPTER 1

WHAT ALPINE PLANTS ARE AND THEIR BASIC NEEDS

One might expect the definition of an alpine plant to be 'a plant from an "alpine" environment'. Up to a point this would be correct. It should be realized, however, that many plants which are grown on rock gardens, or fall within the category of 'rock gardening', are not truly alpine but may be garden selections whose characteristics qualify them for association with plants which actually come from alpine habitats. It is common practice to classify any plants as alpines which are suitable for growing on rock gardens, in walls, stone troughs and sinks, in crevices between paving stones and even in peat beds and walls. Within this generalization there are, of course, many sub-divisions, from the typical, high-alpine cushion-forming plants which are the acknowledged aristocrats to the more ordinary, but no less pleasing, kinds which need no special skills or specially created environments.

The basic needs of alpines in cultivation are neither numerous nor complicated but there is one which is essential to all of them. They demand perfect drainage and will not tolerate soil which becomes and remains saturated for long periods. They like water in plenty when in growth but it must pass rapidly through the soil and not linger in sodden clods around their roots. This important aspect will be elaborated in the section dealing with rock garden construction. If they are grown in pots, pans or other containers, it is a simple matter to ensure that there is good drainage.

The next most important need is the type of compost which is used. Here one must begin by separating plants into two divisions, those which demand or will grow in alkaline soil, and those which absolutely demand lime-free conditions. There are far more of the former than the latter and it is only lime-haters which are completely intolerant. Nearly all the lime-lovers will grow well enough in neutral or even acid soil. With but one or two exceptions, which will be noted where the particular plant is described in later chapters, all plants belonging to the family *Ericaceae* – viz., heathers, rhododendrons, gaultherias, vacciniums etc. – must have lime-free soil. The least tolerant of the lime-lovers are aubrietas, dianthus and many of the silver saxifrages. They will endure but not enjoy acid soils.

The main constituent of any basic compost will be loam, or good top-spit garden soil and it is important that, before it is used it should be tested to determine its pH value. Inexpensive soil-testing kits are readily available from chemists or garden centres. The pH scale runs from nought to 14; a pH of seven can be regarded as neutral, below that the soil is acid, and above seven it is alkaline. A compost which will be to the liking of the majority of alpine plants would consist of two parts of the loam or top-spit soil, one part of fine-grade moss peat (do not use sedge peat, which is very acid) and one part of gritty sand or fine grit. Do not use yellow, builders' sand, which will 'bind' and solidify and not serve the purpose of providing rapid drainage. Should moss peat not be available, leafmould or well rotted garden compost can take its place.

If leafmould is used, ascertain if it has been made from the leaves of beech or other trees growing over chalk. If so it is likely that it will be impregnated with lime. All parts quoted above are by bulk. With the materials assembled, and before mixing them, add a generous sprinkling of bonemeal to the heap. All materials should be slightly dry and not saturated when mixed. Any special composts will be cited under the appropriate headings hereafter. This is the basic and most generally used mixture.

The two generally accepted planting seasons in the open for alpines are spring and autumn, but as alpines are almost invariably pot-grown they can be planted during any season, so long as you can offer the additional care which is likely to be needed if they are planted in the height of summer when periods of drought are a strong possibility. Under such circumstances it is advisable to provide some form of light shading for a few days, and to give a thorough initial soaking. Further applications of water will be needed until the plants begin to make roots and seek their own moisture from the soil around them.

CONSTRUCTING A ROCK GARDEN

To those who hesitate before embarking upon the construction of a conventional rock garden, perhaps because of the lack of a suitable site, it should be said that it is not essential to have a rock garden in order to grow alpine plants. They can be cultivated in several other ways and flourish in wall crevices, in the interstices of paving stones, in stone trough and sink gardens, or even in prepared areas in the front of a flower bed or at a path edge. These are all useful alternatives even though it cannot be denied that a rock garden provides the most suitable and appropriate environment for a collection of alpines.

Whatever project one has in mind, it is as well to have an ideal at which to aim, even if circumstances force some sort of compromise. The ideal site for a rock garden is a gentle slope falling to the south or south-west. It should be fully in the open and not overshadowed by trees or tall adjacent buildings. The fact that the site slopes is a natural aid to the essential good drainage which may have to be artificially created on a flat site.

In the small gardens which are customary today it is unlikely that a site in which a rock garden will merge naturally into its surroundings will be available. It will have to be an arbitrary feature, obviously created for a special purpose. With the site chosen it has to be prepared. All perennial weeds must be carefully dug out and the drainage proven. On heavy clay soils and a level site it may be necessary to make some provision for removing surplus water. For example a deep sump-hole in the centre of the site, filled with coarse material such as broken bricks or broken stone, will greatly help the drainage. Should the natural drainage be good this will not be necessary.

If a local stone is available this should always be used in preference to an imported rock. Not only will it be much less expensive, it will be more in keeping with its surroundings. It is not possible to give a precise estimate of the amount of rock required for a given area, but, very approximately, one should calculate on the basis of one tonne of rock to every 9.3 sq m (100 sq ft). Always use the largest rocks that can be comfortably handled. Very small pieces will not make a satisfactory rock garden. Unless a professional rock-builder is employed the construction is very much a 'do-it-yourself' and personal matter. Do not place the rocks in isolation, try to combine them in outcrops or continuous formation so they appear to be part of a much larger body of rock hidden beneath the soil. Always ensure that the base of every rock is sunk into the soil and that the 'tilt' of all rocks is on the same plane for a convincing appearance.

The compost used should be similar to that recommended in an earlier paragraph and, also as an approximate estimate, reckon on at least 0.76 cu m (1 cu yd) of compost for each tonne of rock. If you build high, with deep pockets, more may be required. Fill each pocket with soil as the construction proceeds, firmly ramming it at the back and sides to ensure that the rocks stand firmly, with no movement. After building and soil filling is completed it is wise to give the whole area a thorough soaking and wait for a few days for an inevitable slight settlement, which should be topped up before planting. Cracks, crannies and crevices are best planted as the building progresses and a few suitable plants should be at hand for this purpose, such as sempervivums, sedums, saxifrages, dianthus, gypsophilas and arenarias. It is difficult to plant such crevices after building has been completed.

PEAT BEDS AND WALLS

It is frustrating for those who have to live with an alkaline soil and wish to grow lime-hating plants to have to deny themselves the pleasure which these plants can give. Given the desire to overcome the difficulties presented by the wrong sort of soil, it is possible to create special areas of neutral or acid soil to accommodate the lime-haters.

Such a project is best achieved by obtaining a supply of peat blocks with which to build walls, or a sort of imitation rock garden, filling the beds thus created with a compost composed of lime-free grit. The proportions, by bulk, should be approximately two parts of peat to one part of soil and one part of sand or grit.

The peat-blocks are used in the same way that ordinary bricks would be used when building a wall. They should be laid in courses ensuring that each joint is overlaid by a block in the course above. It is inadvisable to build such peat walls to any considerable height as they would then lack stability. Bury the lowest course an inch or so in the ground with a very slight tilt 'inwards' so that the final wall slopes inward at the rate of about 2.5 cm per 30 cm (1 in per ft) of height. Additional stability can be obtained by driving a long 15–23 cm (6–9 in) nail through a block here and there into the block beneath. This applies especially to the corners, which are always a weak point in such constructions.

Peat-blocks are not very easily obtained. If you happen to live in or near an area where peat is still cut for burning they should be available, otherwise one must search for a supplier who can provide them. Some specialist nurseries occasionally offer them for sale. After filling with compost and soaking it is important to allow a substantial period for a thorough settlement before planting. If the garden slopes, peat-walls and beds should be on the higher points to avoid infiltration of 'hard' water from above and any artificial watering should be with rain water when possible. The use of chlorinated water from mains is inadvisable except in emergencies. Its occasional use will not be harmful but it should not be consistently employed.

THE ALPINE HOUSE

Once one has been inoculated with an affection for alpine plants, the time will inevitably come when there is a desire to accept the challenge offered by the aristocracy of the race – the high alpines. These ask for, and deserve, special treatment which cannot be given under ordinary outdoor conditions. Not only will the acquisition of an alpine house add a new perspective to gardening; it will also enable you to enjoy a measure of comfort during the winter periods when outdoor work is either impossible or unacceptable.

There *are* custom-built alpine houses which some firms make to a design devised by expert growers, but such firms are few. One which produces a very reliable, well-made and appropriate house is Messrs. Whitehouse, of Frant, nr. Tunbridge Wells, Kent. Failing a specially constructed house an ordinary greenhouse can be adapted. The ideal alpine house has a low 'pitch', which brings the plants nearer to the light than the conventionally sharply-pitched house; it also has ventilators continuously along each side at bench level. It should, where possible, run north and south, with the door at the southern end.

One of the advantages of an alpine house in these days of very expensive fuel is that it needs no form of artificial heating at all. There are those who like to install some simple form of temporary heating which is adequate to exclude frost, but this is not really necessary and is a personal fad. It is not difficult to have some additional ventilators provided in the roof and sides of a conventional house and this is the only essential amendment which needs to be made.

The staging in an alpine house can be one of three types: (*a*) open-slat wooden benches; (*b*) the bench may be covered with sheets of rigid plastic or tin and covered with a layer of sand or ashes; and (*c*) the staging may be made into a 'box' some 15 cm (6 in) deep, which is filled with sand, into which the pots and pans are sunk to their rims. If the latter method is used it is essential to ensure strong bench supports as it greatly increases the total weight. Of the three, the second choice is the one most usually adopted and is very satisfactory. The disadvantage of the first is that the containers are likely to dry out more rapidly, and of the third that plants will quickly root through into the plunging material which makes it less practicable to move them from place to place.

Although the primary purpose of an alpine house is to provide the more temperamental high alpine plants with the shelter they relish from our unpredictable winters, with alternations from cold to warm and from wet to dry – very different from their normal winter sleep beneath a covering of snow – there is no reason why a wider selection of alpines should not be grown alongside the rarities so that there is interest and colour in the house the whole year through. By providing a simple standing or plunge bed somewhere adjacent to the alpine house it is possible to have a regular interchange of plants from within to without and vice versa, thus sustaining the interest within the house. Only the rarer, high alpine cushion plants and some which may not be 100% hardy need be permanent residents, and even the latter will benefit from an occasional 'airing' out of doors during the summer.

The ventilators in an alpine house should be open upon every possible occasion – in fact they should rarely be closed. The maximum of light and air are highly desirable factors in the cultivation of alpines under glass. Watering during the growing season should be liberal but controlled. A good maxim to remember when using a watering can is 'when in doubt, don't'. Plants which have been kept too dry will usually recover, but those which have been over saturated will not.

During the winter resting period very little water will be required; a once-a-week inspection should suffice. When water is given it should be more than a sprinkle. 'Thorough but seldom' might be the maxim for winter watering. During prolonged periods of frost watering will not, of course, be necessary at all and, if there is sufficient warning of the approach of such a period, the plants will meet it more courageously if they are dry on its inception.

Inevitably plants grown in containers will outgrow their accommodation and will need repotting into slightly larger pots or pans. This operation is usually attended to in early spring, or after any particular plant has finished flowering for the season. It may be several years before the slower-growing kinds need such attention, others may ask for it after a couple of years.

In the final chapter of this book will be found a list of suggested alpine house plants from which a selection can be made. It is far from complete, but may provide some welcome ideas to those to whom an alpine house is a new approach in this particular branch of gardening.

CHAPTER 2

PROPAGATION

There are three conventional methods of propagating alpine plants: from seeds, by cuttings, and by division. In a very few cases, of which some of the rarer daphnes and the really dwarf pines are examples, one has to resort to grafting but this is more often used by professionals than by amateurs.

SEEDS

When sowing seeds of alpines it is desirable to give some thought to the nature of the plant from which the seeds have been taken. If it is a pure species it will produce plants identical to the parent plant, or nearly so. If it is a fertile hybrid (not all hybrids are sterile), the resulting seedlings may be a mixed bag. Similarly if the parent is a form or a cultivar, it is unlikely that there will be uniformity amongst the seedlings, from which those which are equal in merit or even superior to the parent, can be selected.

Generally speaking, seeds of alpines should be sown as soon after ripening as possible, a rule which applies particularly to such genera as *Gentiana, Primula, Ranunculus* and *Lewisia*. Seeds from plants in any of these genera can, with advantage, be sown literally from pod to pan immediately they are ripe. It is worth noting that seeds of *Ranunculus* and *Lewisia* may fall even before they appear to be ripe. Another pitfall to be aware of is that nearly all campanulas open their seed pods at the back. Whilst you are patiently watching the front door the seeds may be escaping from the rear.

If alpine seeds have to be stored before they are sown they should be kept in a cool, dry place and, for a week or so before they are actually sown, they will benefit by being placed in a domestic refrigerator. If they are sown in the late autumn, exposure of the containers to frost often hastens germination. If they can also receive a covering of snow, this will be helpful as it is what many of them are accustomed to in their native environment.

Seeds which are attached to long awns, as for example, the seeds of the several species and forms of *Pulsatilla*, the pasque flower, will give a more generous and speedy germination if they are individually 'speared' into the compost and not sown flat and covered with soil or grit. With exposure to warmth and humidity, the awns twist and, by a corkscrew action, drive the seeds deeper into the soil.

Some seeds, of which *Lilium* (lilies) and some gentians are examples, are 'flat' – that is, the actual fertile grain is enclosed in a papery wing. Although it is a rather tedious operation germination will be improved if they are sown edgeways and not flat. This can be done by making a narrow 'trench' in the compost, using a thin piece of wood or metal, and inserting the seeds edgeways into this.

Seeds of dicotyledons when they germinate display two 'cotyledon' leaflets. As soon as these are replaced by the true leaves, the seedlings are ready for pricking off separately. Provided the seeds have been sown thinly, this is a delicate but not necessarily difficult operation. It will be performed with less risk of damaging the fragile roots if the soil has been allowed to become fairly dry.

Monocotyledons, which include all bulbs, corms and most tubers, do not have the two cotyledon leaves and are best left to die down and remain in their container for another year, to be finally handled upon their second appearance, by which time they will have developed their bulbs, corms or tubers. Obviously, such seeds should also be sown thinly. If overcrowded the little bulbils will not have sufficient space for healthy development.

After-care of pricked-off seedlings consists of keeping them under cover in cool conditions, watering when it appears necessary, and finally potting them, or even planting them into permanent positions as soon as they are large enough to justify such treatment.

CUTTINGS

Vegetative propagation by means of cuttings is an interesting and rewarding method of increasing plants of which additional specimens are required. It frequently has to be resorted to in the case of plants which are of hybrid origin, and therefore are either sterile or will not produce plants identical to the parent. Examples are named clones or selections of such genera as *Aubrieta*, cushion phloxes, *Dianthus*, helianthemums – in fact all plants which are not true species.

In the main, cuttings are of two types: soft tips made from young, non-flowering shoots and cuttings made from mature material, which are harder and are often taken with a tiny 'heel' of older wood. These are obtained by pulling them sideways from the stem or shoot on which they have grown. It is sometimes difficult to discover young shoots which do not contain flower buds, but even a certain proportion of these can be persuaded to root if the flower bud is removed, either when the cutting is made or as soon as it develops sufficiently to be nipped out.

Soft-tip cuttings are made by removing the lower leaves and cutting immediately below a joint, or node in the stem, leaving a 'leg' of sufficient length for easy insertion into the rooting medium. Rooting will be facilitated if the base of each cutting is moistened and dipped into a hormone-rooting powder, preferably one which also contains a fungicide. Such preparations are available from most garden centres or horticultural sundriesmen.

Individual gardeners commonly have their own recipes for a compost in which to insert cuttings. With increasing experience it is discovered which compost best suits certain types of cutting or variety of plant, but a good basic beginning is to use a sharp silver-sand or very fine grit. It can be used 'neat', or mixed with one quarter of its bulk of finely sifted moss peat. The peat is a useful addition if it seems likely that the cuttings may not be potted immediately they are rooted, providing enough food for them to exist upon until there is an opportunity to handle them.

Once made and inserted, cuttings ought to be kept in a closed frame or box, with ventilation excluded until they begin to root, when they should be removed and given plenty of air but still with a modicum of protection. Very small quantities, or individual insertions, can be placed in sealed plastic bags until they begin to root. Alternatively, cut in half a plastic bottle in which orange-squash or other soft drink is sold, and one has two useful 'bell-glasses' which will fit neatly over a pot or pan and provide excellent rooting conditions. The screw-top should, of course, be retained for the upper half of the bottle to ensure an airtight container.

A similar procedure should be followed for both soft cuttings and those made from harder wood. The latter will take longer to root and, if made from mid-summer onward, possibly may not root until the following spring. Those who are really enthusiastic propagators may consider installing in a greenhouse a 'mist-unit'. This is an automatic system with spray nozzles, operated either by a time-switch or an electronic 'leaf', which give a fine mist of moisture at periodic intervals. This, on a large scale, is the now commonly adopted commercial practice, but small amateur units are available and are not costly either to install or run. It is advisable to have such a unit initially installed by a competent electrician.

Shrubby plants are usually rooted from the more mature, hard-wood cuttings. Some can be rooted from soft tips, which are always worth trying when available, but the 'heel' cuttings are more certain to give successful results. Treat the cuttings exactly as for soft tips, removing the lower leaves and leaving a 'leg', and remember to trim off the heel of older wood neatly with a very sharp knife but do not cut at a node or joint. It may happen, especially with hard-wood cuttings, that a large callus is formed at the base of the cutting which seems reluctant to produce roots. Should this be so, rooting can often be induced by briefly soaking the callus in a 5% solution of acetic acid, or in undiluted white vinegar.

DIVISION

Many alpine plants lend themselves readily to increase by division of old and established plants, but there are some which make their growths from a single 'neck' or crown and these have to be propagated from seeds or cuttings. The most suitable time of the year at which to make use of division is either in the spring or the autumn or, in some cases, directly the particular plant has finished flowering and is beginning to make new growth.

Very often it is possible to gently 'explore' round the sides of an established plant and discover pieces which have rooted and can be detached. Others will 'root as they go' and such rooted branchlets can be cut off and grown on as individuals. In other cases it is best to lift the whole plant and gently pull it to pieces.

During spring and autumn such rooted portions can usually be planted directly into their new permanent positions, but during mid-summer or in the depths of winter it is advisable to pot them and keep them under cover until sufficiently established to be planted out, giving them, in fact, the same treatment that is meted out to rooted cuttings.

CHAPTER 3

AN ALPHABETICAL LIST OF DESIRABLE ALPINE PLANTS

Acaena *Rosaceae*

This is a race of rampageous carpeting plants, largely native to New Zealand, but with a few escapees in S. America and Polynesia. None of them presents any difficulty in cultivation – indeed, they must be used with the greatest discretion in chosen situations. If planted too near to less invasive neighbours, which they will quickly smother, they can be a decided embarrassment. Their ideal use is as ground-coverers or for planting in the chinks and cracks between paving stones. They are so decorative that, in the proper position they can be regarded as indispensable. They flourish in sun but will tolerate light shade and are completely 'unfussy' about soil as long as it is well drained. A highly spectacular vista may be achieved using drifts of mixed acaenas underplanted with autumn-flowering *Crocus speciosus*. Their strongly spreading habit can prove most valuable in some parts of the garden, however, as they form such effective ground coverers.

A. adscendens. Not one of the dwarfest species and will grow into 23 cm (9 in) tangled mats of blue-grey foliage with heads of creamy-green flowers. The correct name for the plant grown under this name is *A. magellanica*.

A. buchananii. Mats of pea-green leaves and characteristically bristly yellow-brown flowers in dense clusters. The hooked bristles which arm the inflorescences of most acaenas are a particular nuisance to farmers in New Zealand as they become entangled in the sheep's wool as they graze areas occupied by colonies of various species. Fortunately this is one plant that we cannot be blamed for having introduced into New Zealand!

A. glabra. This is an exception, having no bristles on the flower heads, in which the small flowers are attended and ornamented by crimson calyces.

A. magellanica. See *A. adscendens*

A. microphylla. The most commonly encountered species in gardens and to be valued for its creeping carpets of bronze foliage and burr-like heads of tiny flowers accompanied by prominent scarlet bristles. It makes a splendid late summer and early autumn display.

A. novae-zelandiae. This very vigorous species is similar to, but slightly larger than *A. sanguisorbae (A. anserinifolia)*. Both make widely spreading carpets of silky-haired leaves and display heads of purplish flowerlets.

All of the above-named species are natives of New Zealand.

Acantholimon *Plumbaginaceae*

A great many species of this interesting genus are known but, alas, very few of them are in cultivation. They are natives of hot, dry hillsides and mountains from Greece eastward to Syria and even into far Tibet. Their habit is to form massed tuffets of spiky, hard leaves. They are avid sun-lovers and demand sharp drainage and positively enjoy a good summer drought.

A. glumaceum. This is the commonest and easiest species. Its deep green cushions of foliage – less spiky than some – are adorned during summer with sprays of pink flowers on short, wiry stems. Should you be climbing Mount Ararat in search of the remains of Noah's Ark, you may well tread on cushions of *A. glumaceum.*

A. venustum. Although still a rarity, this splendid plant has been culti-vated since it was introduced from the Cilician Taurus in 1873 and was, almost immediately, honoured by the award of a First Class Certificate by the Royal Horticultural Society. It is seen at its best when given alpine-house treatment, grown in deep pots of gritty, but humus-rich soil. The needle-sharp leaves are grey and form loose rosettes from which rise long, arching sprays of pink flowers, encircled by silvery bracts. These bracts persist and are as decorative as the flowers themselves, a fact which is clearly shown in Fig. 1.

Fig. 1 *Acantholimon venustum*

It would be pointless to give detailed descriptions of the many other species, but any acantholimon is worth acquiring and giving VIP treatment. *A. echinus* and *A. creticum* are very occasionally listed in specialist catalogues.

Aceriphyllum *Saxifragaceae*

If American troops in Korea had been able to spare time for other than warlike pursuits they might have seen *A. rossii*, the only member of its genus, growing on moist mountain ledges. It was formerly placed in *Saxifraga*, but is now correctly *Mukdenia rossii*. Rather a rarity in cultivation, it produces from clumps of thick rhizomes rounded, glossy green leaves and 23 cm (9 in) stems bearing umbels of pretty white flowers. It likes a cool position and blossoms in early spring.

Achillea *Compositae*

There are achilleas which are tall plants for flower borders but here we are concerned only with the dwarf alpine kinds, which are all sun-lovers and grow more characteristically and certainly flower more freely if they are given rather spartan conditions in gritty soil. They blossom in spring and early summer but are to be appreciated as much for their foliage as for their flowers.

A. ageratifolia. A Grecian species with narrow, deeply-toothed silver-grey leaves and unusually large white flowers carried singly on short stems.

A. × argentea. Flat mats of intensely silver leaves make this a valuable carpeter, scarcely needing the bonus of small, but very pure white flowers.

A. aurea. Of this species the form known as 'Grandiflora' should be sought. It was discovered on Mount Olympus in Greece. The ferny, grey-green, finely dissected leaves grow in low tufts from which spring 23 cm (9 in) stems in early summer, each one bearing a large head of golden flowers. The type species is a pleasant enough plant but is definitely superseded by this particular form.

A. clavenae. A very distinct and fine species from E. Europe. The oval, toothed leaves are as silver as a newly minted coin and the 15 cm (6 in) stems carry heads of white flowers.

A. grisebachii. The provenance of this excellent plant is uncertain. It is probably a hybrid of garden origin and is to be valued for its carpets of silver leaves and heads of pure white flowers on stems which are unlikely to exceed 10 cm (4 in) in height.

A. 'King Edward'. A dainty and desirable hybrid which is also known as *A. lewisii*. The story behind the synonymy is amusing. It was discovered almost simultaneously in two widely separated gardens many years ago and each discoverer named it, one after his patron and the other after the then reigning monarch. By a few days of priority royalty won the day. Clearly a hybrid between *A. tomentosa* and *A. clavenae*, the marriage has resulted in a prostrate plant with grey-green leaves in flat carpets and tiny clusters of lemon-yellow flowers.

A. moschata. This species, which is of no startling beauty, is included here because, in a race of sun-lovers, it has a liking for a slightly shady situation, where it makes pleasant ground-cover with its tufts of soft green foliage. There is no need to mourn if it does not flower for the blossoms are slightly dingy and unimpressive.

A. nana. Another species which is granted space only for the sake of its smallness and for its very aromatic foliage. Ground-hugging tufts of grey-green leaves and quite worthless, dingy-white flowers.

A. tomentosa. From Europe and N. Asia, this is one of the best known and deservedly popular alpine achilleas. Its leaves are ferny and softly hairy and form dense mats close to the ground over which are flat heads of bright yellow flowers on 10–15 cm (4–6 in) stems.

A. umbellata. A Grecian and another species noted for its oval, lightly toothed and intensely silver leaves. The traditionally white flowers are borne in loose heads on 15 cm (6 in) stems.

A. × wilczekii. Another hybrid of garden origin, probably between *A. ageratifolia* and *A. lingulata*, a taller species not described here as it is too large for most rock gardens. It is possibly the best of all alpine achilleas for foliage effect, growing into foaming masses of silver-grey loose rosettes. The slightly drooping corymbs of white flowers are not unattractive, but do not compare for beauty with its foliage.

Acorus *Araceae*
There are but two species of *Acorus*: one, *A. calamus*, is the tall, bog-loving sweet flag and has no place here, but *A. gramineus* 'Variegatus' is a pleasant little tuft of narrow leaves striped green and white and quite decorative by a pool or stream side – even though an American gardener was once heard to say when shown a goodly tuft 'I guess that wouldn't stop much traffic'.

Adenophora *Campanulaceae*
Close cousins of Campanula and mostly natives of Asia, with a few European outliers. There are several species, some rather tall for the small rock garden. A selection of the most desirable species is given below. Although generally rare in cultivation, they present no problems in open, sunny positions, in good, well-drained soil. They are summer flowering.

A. confusa (farreri). Stiffly erect, leafy stems and loose panicles of deep blue, bell-shaped flowers.

A. lamarckii. Leafy, slightly arching stems and racemes of pale blue flowers.

A. nikoensis. A dwarf Japanese species with short spikes of rich blue flowers.

A. sinensis. Another dwarf, of Chinese origin, bearing narrow racemes of violet-blue flowers.

A. takedai. Bell-shaped, violet-blue flowers on slender arching stems.

A. tashiroi. Quite dwarf and good rich blue flowers, one or few to each stem.

Aethionema *Cruciferae*

The species in this valuable genus are nearly all natives of Eastern Europe and Asia Minor, where they inhabit hot and sunny slopes. Given a warm situation they are easily grown. Although they are lime-lovers they will readily tolerate neutral or even slightly acid soils. The abundant flowers are seen from early summer onward. A short selection of those most likely to be readily available is given below. Those who enjoy gathering together representative groups of certain genera will find others listed in some specialist catalogues.

A. armenum. Low, humped bushlets of entangled woody stems clothed in narrow leaves and terminal racemes of good pink flowers.

A. coridifolium. The type plant is seldom grown, its place in garden value having been usurped by some hybrids which happened spontaneously in a famous Essex garden many years ago. The original discovery was named 'Warley Hybrid' and has been followed by at least two selections of even greater merit. One is 'Warley Rose' and the other 'Warley Ruber'. They are equally desirable and grow as dwarf bushes, seldom exceeding 15 cm (6 in) in height and are smothered with rich rose-pink flowers and are as spectacular when blossoming as a rare daphne.

A. grandiflorum. It sometimes takes a very long time for a really good plant to receive official recognition. Although *A. grandiflorum* was introduced from the Middle East in 1879, it was not until 1938 that it was given the well-deserved Award of Garden Merit. The 30 cm (12 in) bushes of woody stems are smothered with terminal racemes of rich pink flowers from May until August.

A. pulchellum is not unlike *A. grandiflorum* but is a little dwarfer and its innumerable flowers are the colour of pink coconut-ice.

A. theodorum. There is a plant in circulation under this name and it frequently appears in catalogues. There seems to be no official record for the name and it differs little, if at all, from *A. grandiflorum*.

Ajuga *Labiatae*

These rampant ground-coverers may seem out of context in a book about alpine plants. The several named forms are mostly variants of the common bugle, *A. reptans*, a British wild plant. They have their uses in shady corners which they will cover with carpets of foliage, sometimes handsomely variegated, and short spires of blue, purple, white or pink flowers. The best named forms are 'Multicolor' (sometimes listed as 'Rainbow'), 'Pink Elf' and 'Atropurpurea', also a comparative (hybrid) newcomer, 'Jungle Beauty'.

Alchemilla *Rosaceae*

These, too, may seem slightly out of place among alpines, with one or two exceptions, but they also are valuable carpeters for cool places. The ubiquitous but beautiful *A. mollis* is omitted except as a mere mention, for it is far too rampant and coarse growing for the average rock garden. None of them has any special requirements and they are valued for their foliage rather than for flower display.

A. alpina. This really is an alpine plant and is delightful when allowed to inhabit a rocky chink. It forms neat tufts of small leaves which are green above but shining silver beneath. The short sprays of greenish flowers are of little importance. It, too, is a rare British native.

Allium *Liliaceae*

This immense genus presents a problem. Several hundred species are known, varying from border giants to miniatures of a few inches. Just a few of the more desirable plants appropriate to rock gardens are listed below, all of which are hardy and easily grown. They like full sun except where noted and will tolerate almost any soil.

A. amabile. From Yunnan and forms fibrous rhizomes from which rise small tufts of fine leaves and 10–15 cm (4–6 in) stems, each one carrying an umbel of reddish-purple flowers.

A. beesianum really is a treasure. It came from China and, on its erect, 23 cm (9 in) stems, offers pendent umbels of clear blue flowers.

A. caeruleum. Comes from Russia and Asia Minor and is perhaps a little tall, but is nice enough to be admitted. On stems which can attain 45 cm (18 in) are dense umbels of small, clear blue flowers. Among the flowers are sometimes seen a few viviparous bulblets, which can be detached and grown as individual plants. This is a character evident in several *Allium* species.

A. cyaneum. A Chinese miniature emitting from its tufts of narrow leaves, short stems carrying neat umbels of cobalt-blue flowers. It is neat enough to be grown in a stone sink or trough garden.

A. flavum. This should be sought in the variety 'Minus' which carries its yellow flowers on very short stems. It loves a really hot and dry position.

A. karataviense. A bulbous species which produces a pair of large, grey-blue leaves and on erect, 23 cm (9 in) stems large, globular heads of lavender-grey flowers.

A. moly. Any description of this handsome species should, like cigarettes, be accompanied by a warning notice, for it is extremely rampageous. It carries a cluster of rich golden-yellow flowers on 30 cm (12 in) high stems and is superb in a place where it can colonize without becoming a nuisance.

A. narcissiflorum. From N. Italy and S. France and a gem of gems. From fibrous rhizomes rise a few slender leaves and short stems, carrying several pendent, wine-red bells. It dies down very quickly after flowering in the spring and its position should be carefully marked.

A. triquetrum. This is a native species which should carry a similar warning to that issued with *A. moly*, for it is a spreader. It appreciates light shade and produces fairly tall, triangular stems from which depend umbels of large, white flowers, each segment being ornamented by a green stripe.

Alyssoides *Cruciferae*
The two species, *A. graeca* and *A. utricrulatum* are dwarf perennials with attractive yellow flowers, resembling those of alyssum. For dry and sunny places.

Alyssum *Cruciferae*
A race of easy, showy, spring-flowering plants, valuable for providing a bright display early in the year, but to be used in moderation. Once they have flowered they have little to offer for the rest of the year and if grown in large masses create points of disinterest. They are all eager sun-lovers and have no special soil preferences. The most commonly grown kinds are the forms of *A. saxatile*. There are many other species and brief mention is made below of one or two of those most likely to be available.

A. saxatile. This came in its original form from E. Europe, and has been in gardens since early in the 18th century. The typical species grows in bold tufts of hairy, ash-grey leaves over which are short stems, carrying large corymbs of crowded golden flowers. There is a desirable form named 'Compactum', which is dwarfer and neater than the type, and 'Citrinum', whose flowers are lemon-yellow. 'Plenum' is fully double and very showy and 'Dudley Neville' changes the colour of its flowers to orange-buff. There exists a form with variegated foliage but this is likely to appeal only to those who find pleasure in collecting the freaks of the plant world.

Dwarfer, and more 'carpeting' in habit are *A. alpestre*, *A. montanum*, *A. serpyllifolium* and *A. wulfenianum*, all with yellow flowers over mats of grey leaves. The plant often catalogued as *A. spinosum* is correctly *Ptilotrichum spinosum*. It has white flowers on low, somewhat spiny bushes but it should be noted that there are no true alyssums with white flowers.

Anacyclus *Compositae*
A. depressus. A summer-flowering sun-lover from the Atlas Mountains of N. Africa, hardy and easy to grow in gritty soil. From a stout tap-root radiate horizontal, ground-hugging stems clothed with finely dissected grey-green leaves and ending in solitary flowers, of papery substance. The 'petals' are white on the upper side and crimson beneath. Seen with contrasting crimson buds and expanded white flowers it is excitingly beautiful.

Anagallis *Primulaceae*
The well-loved scarlet pimpernel of our cornfields and wastelands is *A. arvensis* and is not a garden plant, but there are one or two others which are definitely garden worthy, including the fine form of another native species, *A. tenella*, the bog pimpernel, cultivated as *A. t.* 'Studland', from the area in Dorset where it was first discovered. It likes a cool, moist position and there will make prostrate mats of frail stems and tiny fresh-green leaves, which disappear beneath sheets of pink, honey-scented flowers in spring and early summer.

A. linifolia. From the warmest and sunniest parts of Europe and N. Africa and not very long-lived. Given a sun-baked situation it will spread into low mats of horizontal, leafy stems and display many large, rounded, gentian-blue flowers. There is a form, *A. l. collina* with flowers of equal size but bright red in colour.

It is advisable to save seeds or take a few cuttings as an insurance against possible winter loss.

Anchusa *Boraginaceae*
Anchusas are usually, and properly, regarded as tall plants for the flower border, but there is one precious species from the highest mountains of Crete, *A. caespitosa* which will fittingly accompany the most aristocratic denizens of any rock garden or alpine house. Dense, hard tufts of narrow deep green leaves grow above a deeply delving tap-root and each rosette of leaves has at its centre a cluster of almost stemless flowers of rich, clear blue.

Androsace *Primulaceae*

Widely distributed through Europe, N. America and Asia, this large genus contains plants for the connoisseur and others for the veriest novice. Those which demand special care and alpine house treatment will be so noted in the following descriptions.

A. alpina (glacialis). This is, perhaps rather naughtily, included because of its beauty, for it is very seldom indeed that it is successfully grown. It was described by Reginald Farrer as: 'The royal rose-pink splendour of the highest shingles', and no one who has seen its mats of soft-haired leaves adorned by myriads of rich pink flowers growing in lime-free screes will lack the urge to 'have a go'. There is no sure recipe for success.

A. carnea. From the European Alps and a choice but easy cushion-forming hummock of dark green tiny thin leaves starred with heads of small pink, or occasionally white, flowers. It has one or two geographic variants, all equally desirable and really differing only in the intensity of the flower colour.

A. chamaejasme. In the Alps this tiny tot likes to be closely associated with other alpine meadow plants and in gardens too, it likes companionship which is not too robust. Its wee leaves are hairy, greyish and pointed and arranged in rosettes over which erupt short stems of flowers, at first white, but becoming pink as they age.

A. ciliata. This is a crevice-loving species from the Pyrenees and should be given royal treatment in an alpine house. On neat humps of leaves which are hairless except for a fine marginal fringe, sit rose-pink, yellow-eyed flowers.

A. cylindrica. Also from the Pyrenees and demanding similar treatment. The rosettes of grey-green leaves crowd into dense domes, on which rest the rounded white, or very occasionally soft pink, blossoms.

A. hedraeantha. Another alpine aristocrat, but not quite so autocratic as others of its genre. It can be grown outside in a gritty scree and has umbels of reddish-violet flowers on very short stems over the dome of rosettes characteristic of this group of androsaces.

A. helvetica. The doyen of high places, always in almost inaccessible crevices, wherein are jammed the neat humps of grey-haired leaves. The stemless flowers are white and yellow-throated. Definitely for the alpine house and feel proud if you maintain a healthy plant; even the experts often fail.

A. hirtella. This completes a trinity of rare species from Pyrenean heights (it should really be a quartet, for *A. pubescens* is yet to come). Tight domes and hummocks of wee rosettes are decorated by the stemless white flowers. Grow it with the other rarities in an alpine house.

A. lanuginosa. This is a very different kettle of fish, hailing from the

Himalaya. It is seen at its best when tumbling from a narrow crevice with trailing stems set with silver-haired leaves and heads of pretty pink flowers.

A. primuloides. A species from the Himalaya which has been grown for many decades in one or other of its several named forms. It was known as *A. sarmentosa* until a botanical 'deed poll' authorized the change. It is doubtful if the original species exists in cultivation but any of its derivatives will serve. There is a close similarity between them, varying only in the intensity of colour of their pink flowers. Look out for 'Chumbyi' 'Salmon's Variety', *A. watkinsii* or *A. yunnanensis*. They can all be grown outside and cluster their rosettes of rather sempervivum-like appearance into dense mats, over which are carried the many-flowered umbels of blossom.

A. pubescens. This completes the quartet mentioned under *A. hirtella*. The pearl-white flowers sit comfortably on the domed hummocks of rosettes.

A. pyrenaica. This Pyrenean species is another cushion-forming plant and is more accommodating than others in its group, but is still to be regarded as an alpine house plant. The minute green leaves form tiny rosettes which build into the neatest of pincushions. Each of the wee rosettes produces one white, yellow-eyed flower. The entire plant can disappear beneath the abundance of blossom, making it a desirable collector's plant.

A. sempervivoides. From Kashmir and Tibet and not at all unlike a cluster of smooth sempervivum rosettes when not in flower. On short stems it bears small heads of clear pink blossoms. No need to shelter it, it is perfectly content in gritty soil and a sunny place in the open air, being used to a rigorous mountain climate.

A. vandellii (imbricata). Under either of its names this is a worshipful plant, to be given a place of honour in the alpine house. It forms argent cushions and pads of tiny leaves gathered into small rosettes and the whole plant disappears in spring beneath a wealth of stemless, white, yellow-eyed flowers.

A. villosa. Inhabits the European Alps and extends into Asia. An easy plant, it makes rather loose cushions of wiry, reddish stems ending in tufts of small grey-green leaves. The white flowers occasionally display a pink centre and are fragrant.

Andryala *Compositae*
A. aghardii is a silver-leaved bushlet, seldom more than 23 cm (9 in) high. It has golden flowers in June and July and will thank you for a hot and dry position.

Anemone *Ranunculaceae*

Our dainty wild wood anemone, whose elegant flowers sway so easily to spring breezes, was given the common name of 'windflower' on the assumption that the name Anemone derived from the Greek *anemos*, the wind. Scholarly authorities have now debunked that pleasant fancy and we are told that the name comes from a corrupted Greek word borrowed from the Semitic and refers to a lament for the slain Adonis, or Naaman, whose blood produced the blood-red flowers of *A. coronaria*.

Anemones of all kinds are found throughout the northern hemisphere and a few have escaped into S. America and S. Africa. The ever welcome pasque flower in its many manifestations, which we have so long known as *A. pulsatilla*, must now be sought in the genus *Pulsatilla*, to which the reader is referred. Another botanical ruling has moved *A. hepatica* into the genus *Hepatica*.

A. apennina. The tuberous rhizome of this charming, spring-flowering species qualify it to be included amongst bulbs, where it is commonly catalogued. The typical plant has flowers like those of *A. nemorosa*, but blue, and there are several named clones whose flowers may be white or pink. It likes a cool, lightly shaded situation.

A. blanda. Like the preceding species this is a tuberous-rooted plant. According to which of the several clones is chosen the flowers may be blue, mauve, white or pink. The best of the blues is undoubtedly *A. b.* 'Atrocaerulea' and there is a quite startling newcomer named 'Radar' whose large red flowers have a white centre. This species, too, prefers a cool position and can be usefully employed as underplantings for shrubs.

A. hepatica. See *Hepatica*.

A. magellanica. Without laying claim to any startling beauty this native of Chile and Patagonia is a useful, easily grown plant for a sunny place, making tufts of deeply cleft, softly hairy leaves, over which stand on erect stems heads of cream-white flowers. The best one is known as *A. m.* 'Major' and is slightly larger, with more significant flowers.

A. nemorosa. The wild wood anemone is not often cultivated, although it could well qualify as a good garden plant. It has a number of named varieties and some of the best are 'Allenii', with powder-blue flowers, 'Alba', white, 'Alba Plena', white and double (Fig. 2), and 'Robinsoniana', with large soft blue flowers.

A. pulsatilla. See *Pulsatilla vulgaris*.

A. ranunculoides. Native of Europe and the Caucasus and commonly named wood ginger. It is a lover of cool, shaded situations where it will wander gently with thin, woody roots from which rise much-divided leaves and short stems carrying golden flowers. It has variants: 'Pleniflora' is double, and 'Superba' has bronzed leaves and larger flowers.

Fig. 2 *Anemone nemorosa* 'Alba Plena'

A. sylvestris. The snowdrop anemone and once much more common in gardens than it now is, more's the pity. It hails from E. Europe and has a running rootstock from which rise tufts of deeply toothed, cut leaves and 30 cm (12 in) stems bearing loose and elegant heads of slightly pendent white flowers. The selected form 'Spring Beauty' has larger flowers (Fig. 3).

Antennaria *Compositae*
Of this widely distributed race there are several species, but few of them are cultivated and some are scarcely garden worthy. Those worth considering here are all forms of *A. dioica*. They are all prostrate carpeters, with silver-grey leaves and small 'powder-puff' heads of tiny flowerlets. The type is white, 'Hyperborea' is pinkish, 'Rosea' is richly coloured and 'Minima' is the baby of the genus with white flowers. They all have their uses as ground cover for small alpine bulbs, or as fillers for crannies between paving stones.

Anthemis *Compositae*
Most of the many species in this genus are too robust for the average rock garden, but there are a few desirable, grey-leaved dwarfs which give a

Fig. 3 *Anemone sylvestris* 'Spring Beauty'

fine and prolonged show of flowers. They are all sun-lovers and grow in any good soil.

A. *biebersteinii (rudolphiana)*. An excellent plant from the Caucasus with low tufts of filigree silver foliage and large golden flowers on short stems.

A. *cupaniana* from Italy is over large, but is so magnificent that a place should be found for a small colony. It makes billowing masses of grey, very aromatic foliage and, the summer through, displays long-stemmed, large white daisy flowers (Plate 1, p. 30).

A. *nobilis*. The common chamomile; not worth growing for its ornamental value in the rock garden, although there is a form with double flowers which is admissible.

Anthericum *Liliaceae*
The more than one hundred species of *Anthericum* are widely distributed and are found in Europe, America and tropical Africa. Two European

Plate I. *Anthemis cupaniana* is a rather vigorous silver-leaved Italian plant, smothered in smart daisies the summer long. Site it where it will not outgrow its welcome.

species qualify as excellent rock garden plants. *A. liliago* is the graceful St. Bernard's lily of subalpine and alpine meadows and is to be valued for the racemes of many pure white flowers which are carried on tall stems over the tufts of narrow leaves. *A. ramosum* is somewhat similar, but a frailer plant and its branching stems carry many white, starry flowers. Both tend to blossom in late summer and relish open, sunny positions in any good, well-drained soil.

Anthyllis *Leguminosae*
The ladies fingers of our own countryside is *A. vulneraria* and is not a garden plant, but there are two selections, *A. v.* 'Coccinea' and *A. v.* 'Rubra' which adorn their prostrate, leafy stems with richly coloured flowers and are worthy of a sunny position.

Aphyllanthes *Liliaceae*
There is only one species in the genus, *A. monspeliensis* which haunts hot hillsides in Mediterranean regions. When seen out of flower it resembles an uninspiring tuft of rushes, but, in midsummer, it justifies its existence by bearing inch-wide gentian-blue flowers amidst chaffy bracts on wiry, 15 cm (6 in) stems. It grows from hard, wiry roots and resents disturbance at any time.

Aquilegia *Ranunculaceae*
A very amoral race, given to hybridization with the result that few of the species can be relied upon to come true from seed, which unfortunately is the only easy way to propagate them, for they do not divide easily or provide cutting material. However, even the bastards are beautiful so that, if you are not fussy about accurate nomenclature much pleasure can be obtained from all the dwarf kinds suitable for rock gardens.

A. alpina. The blue columbine of European Alps, carrying large blue, or blue and white flowers on 30 cm (12 in) high stems – but it seldom breeds true.

A. bertolonii. A dainty pygmy with richly blue flowers on 10 cm (4 in) stems, and it usually comes very reasonably true from seed.

A. caerulea. The state flower of Colorado and a magnificence with very large deep blue and white flowers on tall stems. It seldom breeds true but has bred some fine hybrids.

A. discolor. A Spaniard and a dwarf and it seldom hybridizes, so that its progeny can be relied upon. Over the tufts of deeply divided leaves are 10 cm (4 in) stems bearing elegant flowers of soft blue and cream.

A. ecalcarata. See *Semiaquilegia*.

A. flabellata. This is a Japanese plant, usually grown in the variant named 'Nana Alba'. It is distinct and delightful and almost always breeds truly from seed. The leaves are thick and waxy and grey-green and the cream-white, large flowers are also thick petalled.

A. jonesii. This must be mentioned, although it is the despair of many alpine gardeners. It comes from N.W. America and is a pygmy of no more than an inch or two. Over the tufts of grey leaves should be relatively enormous, short-spurred blue flowers, but it is notoriously shy-flowering. Give it gritty, but humus-rich soil, keep it in the alpine house and hope for the best.

A. viridiflora. This will amuse those who relish the unusual but not necessarily beautiful. A native of China and Siberia, it has green and maroon flowers on short stems. Its lack of startling beauty is somewhat compensated by the fragrance of its flowers.

Arabis *Cruciferae*

In this widely distributed race are several weeds and a few excellent garden plants, varying from easy and showy species for the rock garden to cushions for the alpine house.

A. androsacea. This is one of the rarities from the Cilician Taurus, forming pads of crowded rosettes of tiny grey-haired leaves, studded in spring with short-stemmed heads of good white flowers. Worthy of the alpine house but also flourishes in the open in gritty soil.

A. bryoides. A Grecian with humps of hoary leaves in compact array and white flowers on inch-high stems. A good alpine-house plant.

A. caucasica (albida). This is the common garden arabis, grown in the form of its several named clones, some of hybrid origin. The flowers may be white, pink or red according to kind and there is a good one whose white flowers are fully double.

A. ferdinandii-coburgii 'Variegata'. Flat mats of delightful green and white variegated leaves. The white flowers are unimportant.

Arcterica *Ericaceae*

The one species is a native of Japan. It is a tiny shrublet of no more than a few inches, evergreen, with glossy green leaves on its woody stems, usually arranged in whorls. The pitcher-shaped flowers are creamy-white and appear in small terminal clusters in late spring. It clamours for peat and light shade. The plant has recently been reclassified as *Pieris nana*.

Arenaria *Caryophyllaceae*

A large and confused family and many of the species once included have now been moved to the genera *Alsine* and *Minuartia*. A small selection of those most likely to be available and to please is described below.

A. balearica. No more than a thin film of wee, bright green leaves, all a-dance with multitudes of small white flowers on very short stems. It likes a cool rock over which to spread and will not enjoy being out in full sunlight.

A. bertolonii. Mats of glossy green leaves and quite large white flowers on inch-high stems.

A. ledebouriana. An Armenian species which is nice when planted so that it can foam out of a narrow crevice with tufts of ash-grey leaves on slender stems and heads of white flowers.

A. montana. Another excellent crevice plant which will cascade with woody stems and grey-green hairy leaves. The entire plant can disappear in spring beneath myriads of large white flowers.

A. purpurascens. Arenarias are almost universally white flowered but this species from Spain and the Pyrenees departs from tradition and offers small, soft purple flowers over prostrate mats of leaves.

A. tetraquetra. An aristocrat of the race from Spain and a compact cushion plant well worthy of the alpine house, although it is hardy enough to grow in a gritty scree outside. The minute green leaves are arranged in four-angled array and the stemless flowers are white.

Arisaema *Araceae*
Of this genus containing more than one hundred species only one is included here. *A. candidissimum* (Fig. 4) produces from its large tubers large, three-foliate leaves. The 'flower' is a hooded spathe of white, pink and green stripes. Hardy and easy to grow.

Arisarum *Araceae*
A. proboscideum. This is another aroid and an amusing one which should be established in a cool position to please the children. From small tubers rise low mats of arrow-shaped leaves. In spring many long-tailed olive-green and white spathes seem to plunge into the foliage like mice, leaving their long 'tails' aloft.

Armeria *Plumbaginaceae*
A race of easy-to-grow, sun-loving plants, of which the common thrift, *A. maritima* is the best known example in gardens. They flower in spring and early summer and are decorative and valuable.

A. caespitosa (juniperifolia). A Spaniard which grows in tight tufts of crowded dark green narrow leaves which it adorns with almost stemless heads of pink flowers.

A. maritima. The sea pink of British sea cliffs, grown in gardens in the form of its several named selections, of which the best are 'Alba', white;

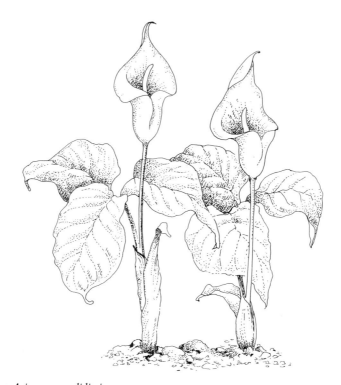

Fig. 4 *Arisaema candidissimum*

'Laucheana', pink; 'Merlin', delicate soft pink; and 'Vindictive', rich red. Also more properly included here is the plant usually catalogued as *A. corsica*, which can be no more than a form of *A. maritima* with brick-red flowers.

Arnica *Compositae*
A small European and N. American genus. *A. montana* inhabits European alpine meadows, always on granitic, lime-free formations. Over its rosettes of roughly hairy leaves hover large golden flowers on 30 cm (12 in) high stems in summer.

Artemisia *Compositae*
Sun-loving plants of little flower value, but appreciated for their grey and silver foliage.
   A. asoana. From hot Spanish hillsides. Mats of deeply cut silver leaves.
   A. glacialis. Tufts of intensely silver foliage.

Plate 2. *Asperula suberosa*, forms tufts of tiny, hairy leaves, smothered in spring and early summer with pink flowers. Height 5–8 cm (2–3 in); spread 15 cm (6 in).

A. lanata. Spreading prostrate cushions of glistening foliage.

A. schmidtiana 'Nana'. Mats composed of circular rosettes of silver filigree foliage. One of the most enticing.

A. stelleriana. A magnificent plant demanding considerable space, forming mounded hummocks of silver-grey leaves.

Asarina *Scrophulariaceae*
A. procumbens (Antirrhinum asarina). From S. France and relishes a cool position, where its trailing, leafy stems will be adorned for weeks on end with tubular white flowers flushed with red and yellow.

Asperula *Rubiaceae*
A. gussonii. Matted tufts of very dark green tiny leaves and heads of flesh-pink flowers on very short stems. Easy in a sunny position.

A. hirta. This Pyrenean species spreads by underground stems. Its lax stems bear whorls of small leaves and clusters of starry, rose-pink flowers.

A. suberosa (Plate 2, p. 35). The aristocrat of the race, a native of Grece and so resentful of winter wet that it should be given alpine house treatment. Prostrate tufts of very hairy, tiny leaves, smothered in spring and early summer with clusters of tubular pink blossoms.

Aster *Compositae*

A. alpinus. From European alpine meadows and a deservedly popular rock garden plant. Above the tufts of narrow leaves are 23 cm (9 in) stems each carrying one large purple flower with a centre of golden flowerlets. Easy in sun and any good soil.

A. natalensis. Although it is a S. African, this comparative newcomer is quite hardy. It spreads in modest mats of hoary leaves and, on 10–15 cm (4–6 in) stems, displays clear blue, yellow-centred flowers.

Aubrieta *Cruciferae*

There are wild species of aubrieta, but they do not match for beauty and garden value the many named clones and selections which are listed in any good hardy plant catalogue. They grow freely from seed but will produce a mixture of colours. The ones with pure colours must be vegetatively propagated and can be chosen to taste from a range of colours progressing from soft blue and mauve, through pinks to brilliant red. They are lovers of sun and lime, flower in early spring, and should be cut back after flowering to keep them tidy and prolong their lives.

Bellidiastrum *Compositae*

B. michelii (Aster bellidiastrum). An alpine daisy of merit. On 10–15 cm (4–6 in) stems are inch-wide flowers whose white ray-florets are often stained pink.

Bellis *Compositae*

The common daisy is *B. perennis*, and neither it nor its several forms, many of them with double flowers, are acceptable rock garden plants.

B. rotundifolia 'Caerulescens', from N. Africa, and hardy, has single daisy flowers of softest blue and *B. sylvestris* resembles the common daisy but its white ray-florets are tipped with crimson.

Berberis *Berberidaceae*

B. empetrifolia (Fig. 5). A dwarf, spreading, evergreen shrub from Chile and Patagonia. It may attain 45 cm (18 in) or more in height and can make a bush of arching branches 60 cm (2 ft) across. The branches are bedecked in spring with innumerable small, bright yellow flowers, which are followed by blue-black berries.

Fig. 5 *Berberis empetrifolia*

Calamintha *Labiatae*
C. alpina. Low tufts of aromatic leaves and, on 10 cm (4 in) stems, whorls of purple flowers in spring and summer. *C. grandiflora* is similar, but a little larger in all its parts and the purple flowers have a hint of red. Both are easy sun-lovers.

Calceolaria *Scrophulariaceae*
C. darwinii. From the Straits of Magellan and an exciting plant, best given alpine house treatment, or treasured in a trough or sink garden. From low tufts of dark green, toothed leaves rise short stems, carrying large solitary flowers of yellow-brown with a startling bar of pure white across the 'pouch' (Fig. 6). As its name implies, this was one of the plants Darwin discovered during the famous voyage of the *Beagle*.

   C. tenella. Is also from S. America and grows as a prostrate mat of fresh green leaves, studded with innumerable short stems bearing small, pouched flowers of clear yellow. It relishes fairly frequent division and replanting, and prefers a cool situation.

Fig. 6 *Calceolaria darwinii*

Campanula *Campanulaceae*

To give this large and very important family the treatment it fully deserves would demand a separate volume and only a selection can be described here. Invaluable for blossoming after the first flush of spring colour is over, mostly easy to grow in open, sunny positions, and extremely decorative, it is a group which should be well represented in any rock garden and in any alpine house, where a few of the more temperamental aristocrats of the race find a suitable home.

C. allionii (alpestris). A lovely high alpine species which demands very gritty soil. A scree is the ideal situation, or a shallow pan filled with scree compost in the alpine house. It spreads slowly by underground stems, emitting here and there tufts of narrow, hairy leaves and on 8 cm (3 in) stems offers large purple-blue bells.

C. arvatica. A Spanish treasure. It loves a crevice in nature, but will be well contented in gritty soil. Mats of tiny dark green leaves are in loose rosettes, from which rise short stems, each carrying several upturned, starry flowers of violet-blue. There is also a nice albino whose white flowers associate pleasantly with those of the type.

C. betulaefolia. A choice and very desirable species from Armenia. On

Plate 3. The massed saucer–shaped blooms of *Campanula carpatica* may be pale or rich blue, purple or white. It makes tufted growth with flowers on 10–23 cm (4–9 in) stems.

the almost woody, semi-trailing stems are wedge-shaped, glossy leaves and the clusters of large flowers appear terminally on the stems. The colour may be almost white to soft pink and the buds are wine-red. It looks well in a crevice and is a good alpine-house plant.

C. carpatica. This is really a group name, covering a number of named forms, clones and hybrids which have arisen from the original introduction in 1774 of this handsome plant. All forms grow as tufted hummocks of long-stemmed, glossy leaves and carry their large, open bell-shaped flowers in profusion on stems which, according to kind, vary from 10–23 cm (4–9 in) in length. The colour may be white, through many shades of blue to rich purple, again according to the particular form which is chosen (Plate 3, p. 39).

C. cochlearifolia (pusilla). This is a daintiness from European Alps. It threads its way happily through any good, gritty soil, erupting into mats of tiny, shining green leaves from which rise short stems bearing the pendent bells. Typically blue, there is an especially desirable albino, and several named forms, such as 'Miranda', 'Miss Willmott' and 'Mist Maiden', all of which have rather larger flowers.

C. formaneckiana. A cliff-dweller from Macedonia and an imposing plant. Its only drawback is that it is monocarpic – the rosette dies after it has flowered and seeds must be sown to ensure replacements. The crinkled, grey leaves are arranged in perfect rosettes, 23–30 cm (9–12 in) across at maturity and acting as a perfect foil to the stately stems which rise from the centre of each rosette, bearing innumerable large, tubular flowers, usually white, but not infrequently tinted or flushed with soft blue or pink. Best grown in the alpine house where it will make a really spectacular specimen.

C. garganica. A variable species with several named forms. They are all splendid plants for crevices in the rock garden or for walls, having stems which radiate from a central crown and hug the rocks among which they love to grow. There is an abundance of star-shaped flowers and these, according to kind, can be white, blue or purple. One particularly good form named 'W. H. Paine' centres its rich blue flowers with white.

C. 'G. F. Wilson'. This is an old, old garden hybrid which has retained all its vigour after many generations of vegetative propagation. From tidy tufts of slightly yellow-green leaves rise short stems carrying large purple-blue flowers of open bell shape.

C. linifolia. A species similar to our native *C. rotundifolia*, the harebell of England and the bluebell of Scotland. A better form named *C. l.* 'Covadonga', which gives profusions of deep purple bells on slender stems (Fig. 7).

C. morettiana. This is a choice rarity for the alpine house, and comes

Fig. 7 *Campanula linifolia* 'Covadonga'

from the Tyrol. It loves a tiny crevice, where it makes little rosettes of softly hairy, ivy-shaped tiny leaves and very short stems, on each of which is one surprisingly large flower of rich blue. Give it very gritty soil and the chink between stones that it loves.

C. portenschlagiana. Also sometimes known as *C. muralis.* One of the easiest and most desirable of its race. It will grow in sun or light shade, hiding its leafy mats of glossy leaves beneath a wealth of purple-blue flowers on procumbent stems. It is an excellent wall plant.

C. poscharskyana. Rampant but lovely. If there is plenty of space over which it can spread it will make entangled masses of long, trailing stems beset with racemes of star-shaped lavender-blue flowers for many weeks. It, too, is magnificent in a wall.

C. thyrsoides. This departs from the family tradition of mostly blue or purple flowers and carries its dense spikes of straw-yellow, fragrant blossoms on upright, 23 cm (9 in) stems.

Cassiope *Ericaceae*

To grow these enticing plants well it is essential to provide them with lime-free soil and a cool position in light shade. They are ideal plants for a peat garden or an equivalent situation. They are low-growing shrublets of the Northern Hemisphere. There is a family similarity between them as they all clothe their woody stems with tiny leaves closely arranged in serried ranks. The urn-shaped, cream or white flowers dangle from thread-like stems which emerge from between the scale-like leaves. One of the best and easiest is *C. lycopodioides*, but anything bearing the name *Cassiope* is worth acquiring if a proper position can be found for it.

Cheiranthus *Cruciferae*
C. cheiri 'Harpur Crewe'. This is the only wallflower which finds a proper home in the rock garden. It is certainly not an alpine plant, but its dense, low bushes of woody stems are smothered in summer with intensely fragrant double yellow flowers. It will be long lived and freer flowering in soil which is poor rather than rich.

Convolvulus *Convolvulaceae*
C. boissieri (Plate 4, p. 43). Better known as *C. nitidus*, (now an invalid synonym), this is a Spanish species which makes marvellous mats of intensely silver leaves, on which rest large, funnel-shaped white flowers. It is happiest in the alpine house and very gritty soil.

Cyananthus *Campanulaceae*
Close cousins of the campanulas from central and eastern Asia. The most commonly encountered, and one of the best, is *C. lobatus*, whose stems spread horizontally, flat on the ground from a central rootstock and are clothed with tiny leaves and end in large, rich blue flowers.

Cyclamen *Primulaceae*
No rock garden could be considered complete without its complement of hardy cyclamen. There are many species; some of them not fully hardy, but a quartet with which to begin would consist of *C. coum*, really a group name for a variable species. It produces its almost white to deep crimson flowers in winter and spring. *C. hederifolium (neapolitanum)* is autumn flowering and can be soft or deep pink or pure white. *C. purpurascens (europaeum)* is summer-flowering and rose-pink to carmine-red, and is sweetly fragrant. *C. repandum* blossoms in early spring and is pink. These four will give flowers for most of the year. All have handsomely marked foliage and like soil rich in humus.

Daphne *Thymeliaceae*
There are short daphnes and tall ones, easy kinds and some which are temperamental. They are highly valued for the beauty and the fragrance

Plate 4. *Convolvulus boissieri*, a Spanish species. Large, funnel-shaped white flowers, borne close to the leaves, appear in summer. Height 8 cm (3 in).

Plate 5. *Daphne petraea* 'Grandiflora'. From north Italy, a slow growing but beautiful dwarf alpine shrub, flowers in spring. Height 8–15 cm (3–6 in).

of their flowers. *D. cneorum* is an evergreen bushlet with dense heads of rich pink blossoms. Its woody stems become partially leafless in time and should be topdressed with leafy soil to conceal their nudity. *D. petraea* 'Grandiflora' could well claim to be the most beautiful dwarf alpine shrub, but it is rare, slow growing and far from easy to obtain (Plate 5, p. 43). In nature it is a cliff dweller, where it forms tangled domes of woody stems sheeted with heads of tubular, richly pink and marvellously fragrant flowers. If it can be obtained it should be treasured and cherished in the alpine house.

D. collina is invaluable where there is need for a rounded evergreen bush up to 45 cm (18 in) in height. It flowers profusely in early summer with heads of fragrant rose-purple blossoms, and there is a less plentiful 'repeat performance' in late summer. *D. blagayana* extends its long, woody stems horizontally at ground level and they end in clusters of cream-white, rather waxy, sweet-smelling flowers.

Dianthus *Caryophyllaceae*
A race of summer-flowering plants whose importance should not be ignored. Generally speaking they are easy and sun loving — with one or two exceptions. There are several alpine species and countless hybrids and selected forms which would require a separate volume to adequately enumerate. As with other large genera only a selection of the best can be included.

D. alpinus. Apt to be short lived, but is easily raised from seeds and is so beautiful that is definitely a 'must'. Flat carpets of narrow leaves are decorated with large, rounded rose-crimson flowers on very short stems.

D. arvernensis. The plant bearing this name in gardens is a dwarf, compact form of *D. gratianopolitanus*. Over its mats of grey foliage are sheets of small, rich pink flowers; there is a handsome albino. A must for every rock garden.

D. deltoides. This is the maiden pink and a rare British native. It should be sought in its best forms, such as 'Flashing Light' or 'Bowles' Variety', both of which have flowers of rich red and crimson.

D. gratianopolitanus (caesius). Inhabits the Cheddar Gorge, where it should be left undisturbed and grown in one or other of its many selected forms, all of which provide low carpets of grey leaves and flowers ranging in colour according to kind from pale pink to deeper tones.

D. knappii. A species which departs from tradition and has clear yellow flowers. It is an untidy grower and is apt to flower itself to death – but it comes true from seed.

D. pavonius (D. neglectus). One of the few species of dianthus which prefers a lime-free soil. Common in the Alps, and a delightful cushion-forming plant with large flowers of soft to deep pink. It can always be identified by the buff colouring on the backs of the petals.

D. superbus. This handsome plant has sprawled its rather untidy way through our gardens since the 13th century. On its lax stems, clothed in broad leaves, are sprays of fragrant lavender-pink, green-eyed flowers. The petals are deeply slashed into a fine fringe and the fragrance is intense.

Dionysia *Primulaceae*
Although these rarities from the dry mountains of the Middle East are very definitely for those with some expertise, they cannot be ignored and are splendid alpine house cushion plants. Of the thirty or more known species, only a few are yet in cultivation. *D. aretioides* has accepted captivity better than most and will make dense humps of crowded softly hairy rosettes, concealed in the spring beneath countless yellow, primrose-scented, almost stemless flowers. Such other species as may be obtainable should be tried and given VIP treatment in very gritty soil, wedged tightly between small pieces of rock.

Draba *Cruciferae*
A race containing many weeds and a few plants of genuine garden value, some choice enough to demand careful culture in the alpine house along with other high alpine cushion plants.

D. aizoides. An easy little tuft of rigid leaves and bright yellow flowers on 5 cm (2 in) stems. Not an excitement, but well worth growing.

D. bryoides. A Caucasian making rounded tufts of crowded tiny green leaves and inch-high, thread-like stems carrying heads of golden flowers. Can be grown outside in a gritty scree, but is happier in an alpine house protected from excessive winter damp.

D. dedeana. From the Pyrenees and has short corymbs of white flowers over cushions of grey-green leaves.

D. mollissima. An aristocrat of the race from the Caucasus. Dense domes of crowded soft stems and tiny leaves disappear in spring beneath a wealth of yellow flowers carried on short stems in small heads. For the alpine house, and water with discretion in the winter.

Dryas *Rosaceae*
D. octopetala. The mountain avens and a rare native of British mountains. Tangles of prostrate woody stems dressed with small, oak-like, deep green leaves and spangled with white flowers like small dog roses. It delights in a sunny place where it can spread its stems over adjacent stones (Plate 6, p. 46).

Plate 6. Mountain avens, *Dryas octopetala*, is a rare British native, common on the Continent. Its tiny rose-shaped flowers are followed by fluffy seedheads.

Edraianthus *Campanulaceae*

A Mediterranean race of sun-lovers, with blue or purple bell-shaped flowers. One of the choicest, ideally placed in a gritty scree, is E. *pumilio*, whose neat tufts of grey-green leaves make a cushion on which rest the violet-blue flowers. Any of the following are desirable, all slightly taller, and equally undemanding: E. *caudatus*, E. *dinaricus*, E. *serbicus* and E. *kitaibelii*.

Erigeron *Compositae*

Apart from the tall border plants there are some dwarf alpine species of *Erigeron*, which are desirable rock garden plants. They are easy to grow and lovers of sunny positions.

E. *aurantiacus*. Perhaps a little tall, as it carries its bright orange flowers on 30 cm (12 in) high stems, but good enough to deserve a place.

E. *aureus*. A treasure from America's Rocky Mountains. Wee tufts of hairy leaves and a summer-long succession of golden daisy flowers on short stems.

E. *flettii*. Also from N. America. It resembles E. *aureus*, but is a little taller with pure white flowers.

Plate 7. *Erodium reichardii* 'Roseum'. The flat pads of mid-green foliage are topped by the pink flowers in spring. Height 2.5–5 cm (1–2 in); spread about 23 cm (9 in).

E. karvinskianus (mucronatus). Admittedly a weed which sows itself all too freely but, as it flowers the whole year through, should be allowed space in cracks and crannies. The flowers are deep pink in bud, ageing to almost white.

Erinus *Scrophulariaceae*
E. alpinus is a pretty little invader which likes to seed itself into cracks and crannies. It is never a nuisance and is quite charming when the neat tufts of small leaves are covered with short-stemmed clusters of pink flowers. The seedlings produce flowers varying from pure white to rich red.

Erodium *Geraniaceae*
These are sun-worshippers from Asia Minor and Mediterranean areas and will thrive in almost any soil. Their prolonged flowering season makes them valuable inhabitants of the rock garden.

E. chrysanthum. Low clumps of silver filigree foliage and branching stems carrying soft yellow flowers. The sexes are on separate plants and the flowers of the male plant are less handsome than those of the female.

E. corsicum. From rock crevices on the sea shores of Corsica and Sardinia. The plant bears grey, scalloped leaves in small tufts of crowded rosettes and pink flowers, the petals veined with deeper colour. It does not like winter wet.

E. reichardii (chamaedryoides). An ever popular plant which came to us first from Majorca in the 18th century. Flat pads of tangled stems with tiny green leaves and rounded, white flowers on thread-like stems. There is a 'Roseum' form (Plate 7, p. 47) and another with semi-double pink flowers. Always worth acquiring are any of the following species: *E. absinthoides, E. carvifolium, E. guttatum, E. macradenum* and *E. supracanum.*

Euryops *Compositae*
When it was first introduced from the high mountains of S. Africa this good plant was named *E. evansii*, but this was later found to be inaccurate. The correct name is *E. acraeus*: a neat, dwarf, grey-leaved shrub of about 30 cm (12 in) in height which carries its yellow 'daisy' flowers in early summer. It is hardy in a warm, sharply drained position and can be featured as a foliage plant.

Frankenia *Frankeniaceae*
F. laevis is a British native and a useful carpeter with flesh-pink flowers, but better still is *F. thymifolia* from Spain, the leaves of which are felted with grey hairs and more richly coloured flowers.

Gentiana *Gentianaceae*

This is one of the most important genera of alpine plants and should be well represented in every rock garden. Unless otherwise stated the selection described below will grow contentedly in any open situation in good soil and, essentially, good drainage.

G. acaulis. This is the big, blue trumpet gentian whose short-stemmed flowers sit on dense mats of congested rosettes of thick leaves. It benefits from division and replanting every third or fourth year. Spring flowering.

G. asclepiadea. This is the willow gentian and its arching stems can attain a height of 60 cm (2 ft). In the axils of the leaves are clusters of pendent blue flowers. It will blossom from July on into the autumn and has a nice albino form.

G. bavarica. This high European alpine, together with *G. brachyphylla* and *G. imbricata* form a group of lovely but admittedly difficult plants. Try them in very gritty, but humus–rich soil. Ideally placed in stone sink or trough gardens or in the alpine house. Their starry, intensely blue flowers are quite exquisite and worth every effort to attain.

G. bellidifolia. This, and *G. saxosa* are two New Zealand species which depart from tradition and carry pure white flowers over tufts of dark green leaves.

G. farreri. This is one of the Asian, lime-intolerant, autumn-flowering species over the mats of fine leaves of which are myriads of Cambridge-blue trumpets. This one is slightly less intolerant of lime than the others in its group but is happiest in lime-free soil.

G. lagodechiana. An easy species but rather confused with *G. septemfida.* Both flourish in any sunny situation and any good soil and, on leafy stems, display heads of rich blue flowers in midsummer.

G. lutea. The giant of the race, its erect stems will tower to a height of 1.2 m (4 ft) or more and carry axillary clusters of straw-yellow flowers.

G. pneumonanthe. A rare native of British heathlands, where it should remain undisturbed and nursery-grown plants sought. 30 cm (12 in) high stems carry tubular blue flowers singly in the leaf axils. It likes a rather moist, but not boggy position, and is late summer flowering.

G. sino-ornata. This can be regarded as the type species of all the Asian, autumn-flowering, lime-hating section. It *must* have lime-free soil and if so given will provide sheets of vividly blue flowers from late August onwards. It relishes being lifted and divided and replanted in March every second year. There are several other splendid gentians in this group, mostly hybrids. One of the very best is G. × 'Inverleith' (Plate 8; p. 50), the enormous blue trumpets of which are quite startlingly beautiful.

Plate 8. *Gentiana* × 'Inverleith'. The vivid blue flowers, up to 5 cm (2 in) long and 4 cm (1½ in across), appear in late summer to mid-autumn.

Plate 9. *Gentiana verna* 'Angulosa'. A rare native, the spring gentian is represented in cultivation by the variety 'Angulosa'. Height 8 cm (3 in); spread 15 cm (6 in).

G. *verna*. A rare native, usually grown in its larger variety G. *v*. 'Angulosa' form. It is spring flowering and is thrillingly lovely when the small tufts are hidden beneath galaxies of starry, deep blue flowers (Plate 9, p. 50). It may be short lived and can flower itself to death after two or three years, so sow a few of the seeds to ensure continuity.

Geranium *Geraniaceae*

G. *argenteum* bears low clusters of cleft leaves, covered with silver hairs and branching stems, carrying rounded pink flowers, veined with deeper colour. A fine scree plant.

G. *cinereum*. From the Pyrenees and of similar stature to the preceding species with deeply cut, grey-green leaves and cupped flowers of a good pink. Its finest manifestation is in the form 'Subcaulescens', the rich crimson flowers of which have an eye of darker colour.

G. *dalmaticum*. Small glossy leaves which adopt rich autumn tints and 10 cm (4 in) stems, carrying neatly rounded pink flowers.

G. *farreri*. From China and a treasure. The large flowers are saucer shaped, clear pink and enhanced by a cluster of sooty stamens.

G. *renardii*. From the Caucasus. The leaves are rounded and velvety, and on short but erect stems are large flowers of pastel-lavender, the petals veined with violet lines.

G. *sanguineum* 'Lancastriense'. Wide mats of leafy stems and myriads of salmon-pink flowers of perfect shape on short stems.

G. *wallichianum* 'Buxton's Blue'. For a cool, lightly shaded place. Far-flung, leafy stems and many large, rounded flowers of soft blue with a white eye (Fig. 8).

Geum *Rosaceae*

G. *montanum*. Clumps of hairy leaves and large, rich yellow flowers on short, erect stems in spring and summer.

G. *reptans*. Not very easy to grow but very desirable. Give it a diet of very stony soil in full sun and hope for the large, rounded golden flowers, followed by seed heads with long silvery awns.

Globularia *Globulariaceae*

A race of alpine shrublets with clustered heads of blue or purple flowers. Any of the following are mat-forming and like dry, sunny positions: G. *cordifolia*, G. *incanescens*, G. *meridionalis*, G. *repens*, and G. *trichosantha*.

Gypsophila *Caryophyllaceae*

G. *repens*. This, and its several named forms are ideal plants for planting in rocky crevices or walls. They hang down their trailing stems and

Fig. 8 *Geranium wallichianum* 'Buxton's Blue'

produce sheets of pink flowers. *G. r.* 'Rosea' has flowers of richer pink, *G. r.* 'Fratensia' is dwarf and neat and *G. r.* 'Monstrosa' is stronger growing and has white flowers.

Haberlea *Gesneriaceae*
G. rhodopensis. For a cool, north-facing or shaded crevice. Tufts of leathery dark green hairy leaves and sprays of open-mouthed tubular flowers of lavender with gold freckling in the throat.

Helianthemum *Cistaceae*
Under the group name of *H. nummularium* are to be found the many named forms, clones and hybrids of invaluable, dwarf, shrubby plants which provide a wealth of colour throughout the summer. They delight in open, dry and sunny positions and should be trimmed quite severely when they eventually cease flowering; this retains a neat and compact habit and ensures longevity. Consult any alpine plant catalogue for a list of varieties. They may have single or double flowers and the colour range is extensive, varying from white, through shades of cream and yellow to

pink and deep red. Some enhance the beauty of the floral display with grey or silver foliage.

Helichrysum *Compositae*
Sun-loving plants, mostly Australasian or S. African.

H. bellidioides. An easy, hardy and pleasant carpeter forming mats of grey-green leaves studded in summer with heads of white 'papery' flower heads.

H. frigidum. An exception in that it comes from Corsica; best in the alpine house. Low tufts of silver leaves and good white flowers (Fig. 9).

H. milfordae. Prostrate pads of crowded silver-haired rosettes on which sit conical crimson buds which expand into large white, paper-bracted flowers.

Hepatica *Ranunculaceae*
Formerly included in the genus *Anemone*. Delightful spring-flowering plants for cool positions.

H. nobilis (triloba). Three-lobed leaves in neat clumps and wide blue flowers. There are rare pink and white forms and some much desired double-flowered forms which are difficult to come by.

H. transsilvanica (angulosa). Similar to, but a little larger in all its parts than the preceding species.

Fig. 9 *Helichrysum frigidum*

Houstonia *Rubiaceae*
H. caerulea. A dainty N. American, where it is known as Bluetts. For a cool situation. Loose mats of tiny stems and leaves and sheets of soft blue flowers in spring and early summer. Plants in cultivation under this name are usually *H. michauxii (H. serpyllifolia)*.

Hutchinsia *Cruciferae*
H. alpina. A dainty and easy lover of a cool position in a rocky chink. Over the low tufts of soft green leaves are quantities of starry white flowers in spring. The sub-species *auerswaldii* is slightly larger with dark green foliage.

Hypericum *Guttiferae*
A genus of sun-lovers without exception, summer and early autumn flowering.
    H. coris. A distinct 23 cm (9 in) evergreen shrublet with tiny leaves in whorls on the woody stems and clusters of golden flowers.
    H. empetrifolium. The most desirable form is *H. e.* 'Prostratum', which spreads its woody stems at ground level, adorned with many rich yellow flowers.
    H. olympicum (polyphyllum). A universal favourite. Its low, mounded bushes are smothered with richly golden flowers for weeks on end. One of the best.
    H. reptans. From the Himalaya and a gem, asking for a sunny spot in gritty soil. Flat mats of leafy stems, each one ending in a large golden blossom.
    H. trichocaulon. Comes from Crete and is particularly neat as a prostrate evergreen. The crimson buds open into bright yellow flowers.

Iberis *Cruciferae*
I. sempervirens 'Snowflake'. If a block of solid, pure white flowers is desired no rock plant is better fitted to provide it than this dwarf, almost shrubby plant. About 23 cm (9 in) high and easy to grow in any good soil and full sun.

Iris *Iridaceae*
Gardeners in general owe a great debt to this great genus which, from the tiny bulbous species to the tall 'flag' irises of the herbaceous border adds so materially to garden beauty. The bulbs and the tall kinds are not included here but there are a few dwarf species which are invaluable for the rock garden.
    I. chamaeiris. A variable European species, often confused with *I.*

Plate 10. Edelweiss, *Leontopodium alpinum*, needs an open sunny position to thrive.

pumila. I. c. 'Campbellii', only about 15 cm (6 in) tall flowers in the spring with large blossoms of indigo-blue.

I. cristata. From N. America and a charming miniature, only an inch or two in height. The lilac and orange flowers have a white crest on the falls. It likes a cool position in humus-rich soil.

I. gracilipes. A Japanese species from mountain woodlands. The slender, branching stems carry several lilac flowers, conspicuously orange-crested. It, too, is for a cool position.

I. innominata. From N. America and variable. The short-stemmed flowers may be clear yellow, or display a variety of pastel shades. It prefers a sunny position but not arid soil.

I. lacustris. A N. American species, similar to, but even smaller than *I. cristata*, and for a similar situation.

I. pumila. Widely distributed in Europe and Asia Minor and immensely variable. In gardens it consists of many named forms and hybrids with flowers of various colours. It is a sun-lover.

I. unguicularis (stylosa). The Algerian winter-flowering iris is a universal favourite. Although not really a rock garden plant its claims cannot be ignored for a sunny position against a warm wall. Its lavender flowers can be picked from November onward.

Jasione *Campanulaceae*
J. jankae. An easy plant making neat tufts of hairy leaves and carrying on its 30 cm (12 in) high stems heads of deep blue flowers in summer.

Kalmiopsis *Ericaceae*
K. leachiana. The only species in its genus and an invaluable dwarf shrub for lime-free soil. A splendid peat garden plant. Round evergreen bushlets with leathery, deep green leaves and terminal racemes of urn-shaped, richly pink flowers in spring and early summer. From N. America.

Leontopodium *Compositae*
L. alpinum. Although not of any conspicuous beauty the edelweiss is a traditional alpine which everyone wishes to grow. It is easily pleased in any open, sunny position. The tufts of grey leaves are surmounted by heads of flowers which seem made of grey flannel (Plate 10, p. 55).

Leucanthemum *Compositae*
L. hosmariense (correctly *Chrysanthemum hosmariense*). From N. Africa, but hardy. Hummocks of woody stems clothed in silver leaves and, all through the summer, a succession of large, white, golden-eyed, daisy-shaped flowers (Plate 11, p. 58). Give it full sun in a warm situation.

Lewisia *Portulacaceae*

A race of N. American alpine plants which have found increasing favour over the past several decades, and particularly since they have hybridized freely and produced several highly decorative strains of spring flowering and colourful plants. Few of the originally discovered species are grown and it cannot be denied that, with a few exceptions, the hybrids are better garden plants. They are not over fond of lime and like to be grown in crevices or on a slope to ensure perfect drainage. They are sun-lovers and appreciate a drying-off period after flowering.

L. brachycalyx. This is one of the few species which has retained its purity. It is deciduous with a thick, fleshy root from which rise, in early spring, narrow, fleshy leaves in rosettes and clusters of short-stemmed large white, multi-petalled flowers.

L. rediviva. Another deciduous true species with a short, thick root from which is emitted a tuft of fleshy leaves and several enormous rose-red flowers.

L. tweedyi. Undeniably the aristocrat of the genus. From clumps of large, wide, leathery leaves rise many stems, each carrying one very large flower coloured in a suffusion of yellow, pink and apricot – difficult to describe but beautiful to see.

L. hybrids and strains. Several named strains exist, all of them offering a fine mixture of various shades of pink, orange, red, crimson and, rarely, pure white. Additionally several hybrids have been selected and given clonal names and are sterile and vegetatively propagated. One in particular is *L.* × 'Pinkie' (Plate 12, p. 59), which is very dwarf and clusters its pink flowers in the centre of a rosette of fleshy leaves.

Linaria *Scrophulariaceae*

L. alpina. The dainty alpine toadflax is short lived but very desirable. In a sunny place it will seed itself harmlessly. The neat tufts of short stems with blue-grey leaves in dense whorls form a setting for the orange and violet flowers.

Linnaea *Caprifoliaceae*

L. borealis. This is the only species in the genus. Widely distributed throughout Europe, including Britain, and in N. America. It is a woodland plant for lime-free soil. The ground-hugging stems have tiny, rounded leaves in pairs, from the axils of which rise short stems each carrying a pair of small but exquisite pink and pendent bells.

Linum *Linaceae*

L. campanulatum. This, and *L. capitatum* and *L. flavum* are three dwarf,

Plate 11. *Leucanthemum hosmariense.* A sub-shrubby species from North Africa. The white flowers 4 cm ($1\frac{1}{2}$ in) across, appear in succession all through the summer.

shrubby flaxes with richly golden flowers, all avid sun-lovers. *L. arboreum* is also shrubby and yellow but is taller in stature.

    L. monogynum. Nearly all linums are blue or yellow-flowered (with at least one red-flowered annual species), but this New Zealander carries on its short, leafy stems, heads of large pure white blossoms.

    L. narbonense. Tall growing with graceful, arching stems which carry quantities of slightly funnel-shaped flowers of rich blue for long summer periods.

Lithophragma *Boraginaceae*
L. diffusum. A trailing shrub from hot hillsides in S.W. Europe, and for lime-free soil. The wild type is seldom grown but there are in gardens two selected forms, 'Heavenly Blue' and 'Grace Ward'. The former is the older and is partially superseded by the latter, whose brilliant blue flowers are a trifle larger and which is more vigorous and easily established.

Lotus *Leguminosae*
L. corniculatus. This is our native bird's-foot trefoil which is cultivated in its double-flowered form. Sheets of yellow flowers on prostrate mats of tangled stems and foliage. Full sun and any good soil.

Plate 12. *Lewisia* × 'Pinkie'. In this very dwarf (and sterile) hybrid the pink flowers are borne centrally in the rosettes of fleshy leaves.

Lychnis *Caryophyllaceae*
L. alpina. Not a plant of startling beauty, but a useful, easily-grown, spring-flowering alpine of modest stature, with neat heads of soft purple flowers. Seedlings quite often produce albinos.

Maianthemum *Liliaceae*
M. bifolium. A dwarf and dainty wanderer for cool places. It dies down for the winter, erupting in spring with many twin, heart-shaped leaves and elegant but short spires of fluffy white flowers. A rare British native.

Mazus *Scrophulariaceae*
M. pumilio from New Zealand and Australia has blue and white flowers, *M. radicans*, also a New Zealander has white and violet flowers and *M. reptans*, from the Himalaya has purple-blue flowers marked with white and yellow. All three are carpeters and the blossoms are almost stemless.

Meconopsis *Papaveraceae*
Beautiful though they are, most *Meconopsis* species are too tall for the rock garden. An exception is *M. quintuplinervia*, only 30 cm (12 in) or so in height, with nodding lavender-blue flowers. It is a good perennial in a cool position.

Mentha *Labiatae*
M. requienii. This tiny Corsican mint makes a green smear on the ground, studded with tiny lavender flowers. It is intensely aromatic and likes a not too hot position.

Mibora *Graminiae*
M. minima. A minute, annual grass ideal for associating with dwarf alpines that relish companionship, of which *Gentiana verna* is a good example. 5 cm (2 in) high tufts of emerald grass.

Mimulus *Scrophulariaceae*
A genus of moisture-loving plants, a few of which are ideal rock garden plants. Most of those most suitable are forms of *M. cupreus* and the following named clones are colourful and easy to grow: 'Bees Dazzler', 'Brilliant', 'Fireflame', 'Red Emperor' and, particularly, 'Whitecroft Scarlet'. An exception to the general rule of a damp situation is *M. primuloides*, a choice N. American, forming prostrate mats of thin stems with yellow flowers on 2.5 cm (1 in) high stems. It likes cool situations, but not a bog and should be divided and replanted every other year.

Minuartia *Caryophyllaceae*
A confused genus containing no plants of startling beauty, but *M. verna* (which can be found in some catalogues as either *Arenaria verna* or *Alsine verna*, and is a very rare British native) makes the neatest of tiny green tufts starred with small white flowers. It is another good associate for plants which like a companion.

Moltkaea *Boraginaceae*
M. petraea. A tidy bushlet only a few inches high, its woody stems clothed in ash-grey leaves and heads of soft blue flowers. The genus is related to, and frequently confused with *Lithospermum*.

Morisia *Cruciferae*
M. monanthos (hypogaea). The only species in its genus and found as a wildling in the coastal sands of Corsica and Sardinia. Flat tufts of narrow, jagged-edged leaves and central, stemless clusters of bright yellow flowers. Give it full sun and very sandy soil.

Nierembergia *Solanaceae*
N. repens. From S. America but hardy in sun and gritty soil. It creeps modestly by underground stems and emits many short-stemmed, large, pure white flowers in summer.

Oenothera *Onagraceae*

A large genus, all of American origin and mostly too tall for the rock garden, but *O. acaulis* makes a dandelion-leaved tuft, centred by white or yellow flowers. *O. caespitosa* is a magnificence from desert areas with huge and fragrant white flowers. Best grown in the alpine house.

O. missouriensis is a lush plant making wide, low tangles of leafy stems and carrying a summer-long succession of very large yellow flowers.

Omphalodes *Boraginaceae*

O. cappadocica and *O. verna* are two early spring flowering delights for cool positions with showers of clear blue flowers on short stems. *O. verna* also has a charming albino. *O. luciliae* comes from cliffs in Greece and is a fine alpine house plant with blue-grey, rather waxy leaves and branching stems bearing china-blue flowers. It loves gritty soil rich in lime.

Onosma *Boraginaceae*

O. taurica has narrow, roughly hairy leaves and is a fine crevice plant. The yellow, fragant flowers are carried in pendent clusters in summer.

Origanum *Labiatae*

A race of sun-loving, semi-shrubby plants of dwarf stature carrying their small flowers amongst colourful bracts. Of particular merit are the Cretan dittany, *O. dictamnus* with felted silver foliage, and *O. rotundi-*

Fig. 10 *Origanum rotundifolium*

folium (Fig. 10) the whorls of soft pink flowers of which are largely hidden by large, pale green bracts. Although reasonably hardy they are probably happier in the alpine house.

Oxalis *Oxalidaceae*

A large genus with a world-wide distribution, all sun-lovers. A few of the most desirable are described below.

O. adenophylla. From S. America. From scaly, soft tubers rise crinkled, silver leaves and large, white to rose-pink flowers in spring.

O. enneaphylla. From the Falkland Islands. Chains of scaly tubers emit silvery leaves and large flowers which may be white or flushed pink. It likes soil rich in humus.

O. lobata. The curious habits of this Chilean species need to be known. In the spring it sends up from a tiny tuber a cluster of bright green leaves. These very soon disappear and nothing more is seen until the autumn, when they reappear, but this time accompanied by many brilliantly golden flowers on 8 cm (3 in) stems.

Papaver *Papaveraceae*

P. alpinum. The exquisite, but short-lived alpine poppy is best regarded as an annual or biennial and it should be allowed to seed itself, as it will do, quite inoffensively. Neat little round poppy flowers rest atop 10 cm (4 in) stems and may be white, pink or yellow.

Paradisea *Liliaceae*

P. liliastrum. This, the St. Bruno's lily, is the only species in its genus and it inhabits European alpine meadows. From vigorous tufts of narrow leaves rise tall stems bearing short spikes of fragrant, white flowers like small lilies.

Parnassia *Saxifragaceae*

P. palustris. Our native grass of Parnassus is worthy of a place in a dampish situation, where it will make neat tufts of heart-shaped leaves. On short stems are heads of white flowers, the petals delicately veined with green stripes.

Penstemon *Scrophulariaceae*

Almost exclusively an American genus, containing a number of dwarf, semi-shrubby plants of great merit. They all like to be in open, sunny positions and are content in any good, well-drained soil with perhaps a slight preference for those not having a high lime content. They are spring and summer flowering. There is much similarity in their general

Plate 13. 'Temiscaming' is the most brilliantly coloured *Phlox subulata* hybrid.

appearance so that individual descriptions, apart from flower colour, would not be very helpful. Any of the following will give pleasure: *P. eriantherus (cristatus)*, purple-red; *P. heterophyllus*, blue; *P. menziesii*, very dwarf, violet-blue; *P. pinifolius*, scarlet; *P. roezlii*, rose-red; *P. scouleri*, purple and a nice albino.

Petrocallis *Cruciferae*
P. pyrenaica. A treasure from the high European Alps, but rather temperamental. Give it a stony scree in full sun and hope that it will cover its low hummocks with fragrant lilac flowers in early spring.

Phlox *Polemoniaceae*
An all-American family, containing among its dwarf, cushion-forming species many very desirable rock garden plants. Unless otherwise stated they are easily pleased in sunny positions and any good garden soil and they blossom in the spring, and then off and on during the summer.

P. adsurgens. This is one of the exceptions and likes a cool, possibly lightly shaded place in soil rich in humus. Tangled mats of woody stems and salmon-pink flowers.

P. amoena. On 23 cm (9 in) stems appear heads of flowers varying in colour from pink to purple.

P. 'Chattahoochee'. A newcomer to our gardens, and a natural hybrid discovered on the banks of the river, the name of which it bears. Erect stems carry innumerable heads of deep violet, purple-eyed flowers. It should be given a cool position and rich soil.

P. douglasii. An immensely variable, cushion-forming species with many named selections, all desirable and ranging in flower colour to kind from white to deep pink.

P. subulata. Commonly known as the moss phlox, this variable species has also hybridized, notably with *P. douglasii* and there exists a wealth of named plants, all colourful, neat and easily grown and prominent in the spring and early summer display. Any good alpine plant catalogue will reveal a lengthy list from which to choose (Plate 13, p. 63).

Physoplexis *Comosa. Campanulaceae (Phyteuma comosum)*
From limestone crevices in the E. and S.E. Alps. Tufts of kidney-shaped basal leaves from which short stems rise, adorned with narrow, lance-shaped leaves and heads of claw-shaped, long-tubed blue flowers. It is a distinctly odd and remarkably beautiful plant.

Pinguicula *Lentibulariaceae*
Most of these interesting and often beautiful insectivorous plants are

rather less than hardy, but *P. grandiflora*, wild in Europe and parts of Ireland, is perfectly hardy in a boggy position. In winter it dies back to a tiny bud, the position of which should be carefully marked. Rosettes of fleshy, sticky leaves, to which insects adhere and are gradually absorbed, and wide-mouthed flowers of violet-blue.

Pleione *Orchidaceae*

Understandably popular, these near-hardy, terrestrial orchids are ideal subjects for growing in pans of humus-rich soil in an alpine house or cold greenhouse. They need no artificial heat or special composts and make a splendid display in the spring. After they have flowered and as the foliage begins to die away, water should be gradually withheld and the pseudobulbs kept dry during their resting period. Watering should recommence as soon as the flower buds can be seen emerging from the sides of the pseudobulbs.

P. formosana (now *P. bulbocodioides*). This exists in numerous forms, some with fancy clonal names. The pseudobulbs are green and the flower colour varies from pure white through many shades of pink and purple with prettily marked throats and lips. It thrives outside in sheltered sites.

P. limprichtii. Is really a dark form of *P. formosana* and one of the most handsome and also one of the hardiest of them all and can be grown in the open in a cool place and with peaty soil. The flowers are a brilliant purple-red with a white throat freckled crimson.

P. pricei. This also is really part of the *P. formosana* complex but always has black-purple pseudobulbs. It is sometimes listed as 'Oriental Splendour' and incorrectly as 'Oriental Grace'.

Polygala *Polygalaceae*

P. chamaebuxus. A tiny alpine shrublet with woody stems and box-like leaves. The short racemes of flowers are yellow and cream, and there is a good form 'Grandiflora', in which the colouring is carmine and yellow. Give it peaty soil and light shade.

Polygonum *Polygonaceae*

P. vaccinifolium (Fig. 11). An invaluable late-flowering plant with trailing stems and tiny, hard leaves which adopt fine autumn tints and sprays of heather-pink flowers. For almost any situation or soil, but not in deep shade.

Potentilla *Rosaceae*

A large and valuable genus of summer-flowering and sun-loving plants, ranging from tallish shrubs to prostrate alpine plants.

Fig. 11 *Polygonum vaccinifolium*

P. alba. Mat forming with dark green leaves and many large, pure white flowers.

P. aurea. Also mat forming with procumbent stems which carry loose clusters of golden flowers. There is also a handsome varient with fully double flowers.

P. megalantha. Tufts of large, hairy leaves and large, richly golden flowers on 15–23 cm (6–9 in) stems.

P. nitida. From the high mountains of Europe, forming mats of silver leaves on which rest almost stemless pink flowers. It demands very gritty soil and full sun and flowers more freely if poorly nourished .

P. × tonguei. A hybrid whose spreading stems form wide mats and emit stems carrying a long succession of flowers the apricot colour of which is suffused with crimson.

Primula *Primulaceae*

P. allionii. There is no more beautiful spring-flowering, alpine-house plant than this primula from the Maritime Alps. It grows into mounded domes of crowded rosettes of softly hairy leaves on which rest countless rounded flowers, the overlapping petals of which are coloured rich, pure pink. It likes to be grown in narrow crevices between pieces of rock and to be given gritty soil rich in humus.

Plate 14. *Primula marginata*, a crevice-loving species from the maritime Alps, is treasured alike for its silver-edged serrated leaves and its handsome heads of lavender-coloured flowers.

P. auricula. The European alpine auricula has rosettes of slightly fleshy leaves, which may or may not have a covering of white farina, and heads of tubular, yellow, white-throated flowers on short stems. It varies considerably, depending upon the particular area in which it originated.

P. farinosa. Our native bird's-eye primula, which inhabits moist northern meadows. Tiny tufts of farinose leaves and neat heads of pink, yellow-eyed flowers in spring.

P. frondosa. From eastern Europe and can be regarded as a robust form of *P. farinosa* with farina on the undersides of the leaves and heads of rose-red flowers, frequently with a white eye.

P. hirsuta. A variable but lovely species with rosettes of hairy leaves and umbels of flowers ranging from pink to clear red.

P. juliae. Originally introduced, many years ago, from the Caucasus and now almost submerged in a wealth of hybrids grouped under the name of *P. × juliana (pruhoniciana)*. They are all mat forming and their primrose flowers may be any colour from white through cream to pink, purple and almost red. They prefer cool positions.

P. latifolia (viscosa). As variable as *P. hirsuta*, and often confused with that species but the leaves are longer, usually narrower. The clusters of funnel- or bell-shaped flowers may be purple or deep violet and are commonly fragrant.

P. marginata (Plate 14, p. 67). A crevice-loving species from the Maritime Alps. Lovely leaves, often silver-edged and notched and heads of rounded pink or lavender flowers. There are many named varieties, perhaps the loveliest being *P.* 'Linda Pope' which has handsome foliage and umbels of large lavender-blue flowers.

P. minima. The Lilliput of the family forming pads of tiny rosettes on which sit almost stemless, surprisingly large pink flowers, each petal notched at the tip.

P. × pubescens. This is a collective name covering a vast array of hybrids and named clones of infinite variety, originating in hybrids between *P. auricula* and *P. rubra* but now enriched by a multitude of garden-raised seedlings. A good example of their excellence is seen in *P. × p*. 'Rufus' (Plate 15, p. 70).

P. vulgaris. This is our own beloved primrose and of this too, there are many variants with single or double flowers of various colours. An especially charming variant is *P. v. sibthorpii* from the Eastern Alps, whose flowers are clear pink.

Ptilotrichum *Cruciferae*

P. spinosum. This is commonly catalogued as *Alyssum spinosum*. It makes a low, spiky, grey bushlet of 23 cm (9 in) or so smothered with white or soft pink flowers. It is an avid sun-lover for any good, sharply drained soil.

Pulsatilla *Ranunculaceae*

This used to be *Anemone pulsatilla*, the popular pasque flower, of which one form is a rare British native. Now correctly named *P. vulgaris*, it exists as a race of many variants with flowers ranging from white to shades of pink and purple to deep red, carried over low mounds of deeply cut foliage. They all delight in limy soil and full sun (Plate 16, p. 70).

Ramonda *Gesneriaceae*

R. myconi. For cool, north-facing or shaded crevices, where it can spread the flat rosettes of roughly hairy leaves, from which are emitted stems carrying wide-petalled flowers of purple-blue. Spring and summer flowering.

Ranunculus *Ranunculaceae*

An important family, widely distributed. It contains many unwelcome weeds but also numerous, admirable rock garden plants.

R. alpestris. A tiny alpine buttercup with wee tufts of lobed leaves and rounded pure white flowers on very short stems.

R. amplexicaulis. Narrow, stem-clasping grey-green leaves and 15–23 cm (6–9 in) stems each carrying several large white flowers.

R. calandrinioides. From the Atlas Mountains of N. Africa and a gem. Very early flowering, often bearing its large, white or soft pink flowers in mid-winter. It is hardy, but the petals are fragile and it is seen at its beautiful best in the alpine house.

R. ficaria. This is the ubiquitous lesser celandine of our roadsides, and should never be allowed entry into the garden, but there are several selected and trustworthy forms, of which one of the most notable is *R. f.* 'Aurantiaca' with flowers of coppery-orange. There are also singles and doubles in white, cream and yellow.

R. montanus. Best grown in its selected form 'Molten Gold'. Neat tufts of green leaves and a galaxy of short-stemmed golden flowers.

Raoulia *Compositae*

Mostly from New Zealand and containing some easy to grow and some rather difficult cushion-forming plants. Give them gritty soil and full sun and where possible some protection against winter wet.

R. australis. One of the easiest and a useful ground-cover for small

Plate 15. *Primula* × *pubescens* 'Rufus'. A hybrid with striking, deep terracotta-red flowers, each having a distinct eye. Height 8–15 cm (3–6 in).

Plate 16. *Pulsatilla vulgaris* produces magnificent gold-centred purple, pink, red or white flowers at Easter time, followed by quaint fluffy seedheads.

Plate 17. *Salix* × *boydii*. Unlike most other dwarf willows which are prostrate, this plant slowly makes an erect bush of gnarled stems and silver grey leaves.

alpine bulbs. Flat mats of intensely silver tiny leaves and many dense heads of minute yellowish flowers.

R. glabra. The easiest of all. Prostrate pads of green and stemless heads of cream-white flowers.

R. hookeri. In effect a slightly more robust and even more silvery *R. australis.*

R. lutescens. A film of tightly packed minute rosettes of grey-green leaves studded with countless heads of minute yellow flowers in spring worth closer examination with a hand lens.

Rhodohypoxis *Hypoxidaceae*
R. baurii. A tiny bulb from the Drakensberg mountains of S. Africa, but hardy in all but exceptionally wet and cold gardens. In early spring it emits clusters of small, narrow leaves and a summer-long succession of short-stemmed flowers, ranging from white through shades of pink to deep red (Fig. 12).

Rubus *Rosaceae*
R. arcticus. A creeper for cool positions and peaty soil. It wanders here and there, displaying intermittent tufts of trifoliate leaves and short stems each carrying one rich pink flower.

Fig. 12 *Rhodohypoxis baurii*

Sagina *Caryophyllaceae*

S. glabra. An easy and useful carpeter, best grown in the form 'Aurea' which forms mats of fine golden shoots, decorated with stemless white flowers in spring/early summer.

Salix *Salicaceae*

There are a great many dwarf willows invaluable as rock garden shrubs. They are all woody-stemmed, mostly almost prostrate – sometimes completely so — and are adorned in spring with fluffy catkins. *S. × boydii* (Plate 17, p. 82) is an exception in that it makes, very slowly, an erect bush of gnarled stems and has not insignificant, cream-puff catkins. From the multitude of others any of the following will be found enticing: *S. apoda, S. arbuscula, S. herbacea, S. myrtilloides, S. repens, S. reticulata, S. retusa* and *S. serpyllifolia.*

Salvia *Labiatae*

S. argentea. Inhabits cliff faces and rocky crevices in E. Europe. Rosettes of large, lobed leaves felted with a dense mat of silver hairs. Innumerable white, hooded flowers adorn a tall candelabrum of horizontal, branching stems.

Samolus *Primulaceae*
S. repens. A frail but attractive plant from Australasia. Creeping habit and slender, 10cm (4in) stems ending in clusters of starry pink flowers.

Sanguinaria *Papaveraceae*
S. canadensis. The Canadian bloodroot is a plant to be treasured in a peat bed or a cool, shaded position in humus-rich soil. In early spring it unfolds from its thick root wide, lobed, grey-green leaves, encircling the buds which expand into pure white flowers. It has also a desirable form with fully double flowers.

Saponaria *Caryophyllaceae*
S. ocymoides. An easy to grow and showy plant, ideally to be placed so that it flows from rocky crevices in rock gardens or walls, bearing cascades of rich pink flowers in spring and early summer. There is a desirable, very compact, flat-growing form named 'Rubra Compacta' which makes a prostrate cushion sheeted with rich pink blossoms.

Saxifraga *Saxifragaceae*
To adequately describe the innumerable species, forms and hybrids contained in this enormous family would occupy more than the pages in this book. For those who are interested in the genus and wish to obtain more detailed information there is an excellent monograph by Winton Harding, published by the Alpine Garden Society.

The genus is divided botanically into a number of sections, one of which is the *Dactyloides* group or, in common parlance, the mossy saxifrages. These are all easy and colourful plants, mostly garden hybrids and selections. They prefer positions which, whilst open and unshaded, are not exposed to baking sunshine. Their name is legion and they will be found listed under their cultivar names in catalogues of rock garden and alpine plants.

Those listed below can only be regarded as a sample of the best and most desirable with which to form a nucleus collection. Unless otherwise stated they all like full exposure and are hardy with a preference for alkaline soil, although they will tolerate other media if necessary.

S. aizoides. Widely distributed from Britain, through Europe to N. America and Asia and an exception in that it likes a cool, moist situation. Mats of narrow, fleshy leaves and yellow, red-spotted flowers in profusion.

S. aizoon (paniculata). A species so variable in its wide distribution that it is impossible to select one particular plant as the typical species. They all form cushions of compact, hard-leaved rosettes and the flowers are almost universally white or cream, with two exceptions. *S. a.* 'Lutea' has yellow flowers, and those of *S. a.* 'Rosea' are pink.

S. × apiculata. a useful hybrid, very early flowering, with soft yellow flowers in clusters on short stems. It also has a nice variant with white blossoms.

S. 'Bob Hawkins'. This is a comparatively recent addition to the mossy group, forming carpets of deeply-cleft, prettily variegated leaves in tones of silver and green. The flowers are white.

S. 'Boston Spa'. Similar in habit to *S. × apiculata* but slightly more robust and the flowers are of a richer yellow.

S. burseriana. A variable species from the Eastern Alps. All forms make domed cushions of congested, hard, silver-grey leaves and carry their large white flowers on very short, usually pink or red stems. A few of the more desirable forms are 'Gloria', 'His Majesty' and *S. b. crenata.* There is also one with yellow flowers, probably a hybrid, named *S. b.* 'Lutea'. They all like very gritty soil.

S. caesia. Mere scabs of congested tiny rosettes of grey leaves and white flowers.

Fig. 13 *Saxifraga cuscutiformis*

S. *callosa (lingulata)*. Another variable species. Compact rosettes of narrow, silver leaves and arching plumes of white flowers. Very good crevice or wall plants.

S. *cochlearis*. Compressed mounds of tightly packed silver rosettes and plumes of white flowers on short stems. There are 'Minor' and 'Major' forms.

S. *cotyledon*. Occurs in several geographic forms throughout Europe and even into N. America. Wide, strap-shaped leaves in symmetrical rosettes and long, arching sprays of white flowers, the petals frequently heavily red-spotted.

S. *cuscutiformis*. A distinct and entrancing plant with wide, scalloped leaves in generous tufts and tall, branching stems carrying myriads of butterfly-like white flowers (Fig. 13). For a cool position and late summer flowering.

S. 'Esther'. A useful hybrid between S. *aizoon* 'Lutea' and S. *cochlearis*, with good heads of cream-yellow flowers.

S. *fortunei*. A distinct species from Asia. It flowers in autumn and on into the winter months and likes a cool position, even slightly shaded. Clumps of wide, lobed leaves, green above and crimson beneath. The elegant branching stems bear clouds of white flowers, the one or two lower petals of which are much longer than the upper ones.

S. *granulata*. This is the British meadow saxifrage and should be cultivated in its desirable form with fully double white flowers. It grows from tiny bulbils and dies down very quickly after flowering in the summer. Not too hot and dry a situation.

S. *grisebachii*. For the alpine house. Symmetrical silver rosettes and crimson croziers formed by bracts amidst which are the small flowers. A very desirable species.

S. *irvingii*. A minute and very early flowering cushion plant; its pads of congested, tiny grey-green leaves are spangled liberally with pink flowers. S. *jenkinsae* is very similar but the flowers have slightly longer stems.

S. 'Kathleen Pinsent'. A meritorious hybrid with long and elegant sprays of soft pink flowers.

S. *latepetiolata*. A monocarpic but handsome species from Spain. Rosettes of kidney-shaped leaves and 30 cm (12 in) high stems bearing myriads of pure white flowers. Save a few seeds for continuity.

S. *lilacina*. From the Himalaya. This saxifrage appreciates gritty soil and a cool position; not one of the easiest but delightful when the flat pads of crowded rosettes are adorned by the almost stemless lilac flowers.

S. *longifolia*. The species come from the Pyrenees, where it adorns sheer cliff faces with plumes of white flowers rising from symmetrical

Fig. 14 *Saxifraga longifolia* 'Tumbling Waters'

rosettes of grey leaves. It is seen as its magnificent best in the hybrid *S. l.* 'Tumbling Waters' (Fig. 14). Give it a sunny crevice and remember that it is monocarpic, but there are usually non-flowering side rosettes which can be detached and rooted.

S. oppositifolia. A rare British native and also found throughout Europe, in N. America and the Himalaya in one or other of its several geographic variants. Prostrate mats of thin stems on which the tiny leaves are arranged in opposite pairs. Purple-red flowers in very early spring. The best selected garden form is *S. o.* 'Splendens'.

S. retusa. From the high European alps and resembles a compact *S. oppositifolia* but its small, rich red flowers are carried in tiny, erect corymbs.

S. umbrosa. This is the name commonly given to our old friend London pride, but it is now inaccurate and should be known as *S. × urbium.* It is a complex group of many variations, the best for the rock garden being those named *S. u. primuloides*, a small group containing several, very dwarf and elegant plants, for cool places, with short stems carrying showers of pink flowers.

Scabiosa *Dipsacaceae*
S. columbaria 'Alpina' (*S. alpina* and *S. alpina nana* of catalogues). A neat and tidy hummock of grey, cut-edged foliage and 15 cm (6 in) stems carrying heads of lavender-coloured flowers. Easy to grow in full sun.

Scleranthus *Caryophyllaceae*
S. biflorus and *S. uniflorus* are two Southern Hemisphere, cushion-forming plants without floral value, but they both make tight, compact, rounded hummocks of compressed tiny leaves. They are ideal sink and trough plants.

Scutellaria *Labiatae*
Few of the many scutellarias are rock garden plants, but *S. scordiifolia* is an exception. A native of Korea, it spreads mildly with wandering roots and erupts with tufts of narrow leaves and 23 cm (9 in) stems carrying many flowers of rich indigo-blue in summer.

Sedum *Crassulaceae*
Almost without exception the members of this enormous family are sun-lovers and will survive in conditions of considerable austerity, but they will also show their appreciation of good living conditions. This is particularly true of the common wall pepper, *S. acre*, which should be avoided in any situation where an immensely vigorous spreader is not desired. Space forbids mention of all but a selected minimum of the most desirable kinds. This, too, is a genus demanding a volume of its own if true justice is to be given to a very popular group of plants.

S. album. Another species which can be a menace, although it has its uses as ground-cover for sunny places where the soil is poor. Several of its forms, such as *micranthum* and *murale* 'Coral Carpet' are better behaved, forming mats of colourful foliage.

S. caeruleum. This is one of the few admissible annuals to the rock garden. A native of Corsica, it grows in neat tufts, smothered in summer with myriads of tiny blue flowers. It self-seeds inoffensively.

S. cauticolum. A Japanese species which is invaluable in the late summer and autumn. Its woody stems, clothed in blue-grey, fleshy leaves end in heads of crimson flowers. It is an ideal occupant of a sunny crevice.

S. humifusum. A Mexican, and not fully hardy, but a good alpine house plant. It likes a moisture-holding soil and stars its mossy tufts with large flowers of clear gold, carried on very short stems.

S. lydium. Easy and desirable, forming the neatest of rounded hummocks of crowded, tiny green leaves, turning red in autumn and winter. Small heads of white flowers on very short stems.

S. oreganum. From N. America and desirable. On its erect, 5 cm (2 in) stems are fleshy, rounded leaves of bronze-red, forming carpets which admirably set off the heads of yellow flowers.

S. primuloides. A Himalayan, making prostrate pads of dark green leaves, studded with surprisingly large white, bell-shaped flowers.

S. pulchellum. A hardy N. American and an exception in that it likes a cool, moist situation. Spreading, prostrate stems have narrow green leaves and the flowers, arranged in the shape of a starfish-shaped head, are pink and are carried during mid- and late summer.

S. spathulifolium. The several forms of this N. American species compose one of the most popular groups of sedums. They all make mats of fleshy, rounded leaves, usually purple and green and often dusted with a white farina. The slightly trailing flower stems carry heads of yellow flowers. The varieties to seek are 'Purpureum' which has leaves suffused with purple and 'Cape Blanco' ('Cappa Blanca'), grey-white.

Plate 18. *Sempervivella alba.* A Himalayan making tufts of green, fleshy leaves and producing short sprays of white flowers. Rosettes 2.5 – 3 cm ($1-1\frac{1}{4}$ in) across.

Semiaquilegia *Ranunculaceae*
S. adoxioides. Almost an aquilegia, and sometimes listed as *Aquilegia ecalcarata.* A dainty Chinese plant with pretty foliage and branching 23–30 cm (9–12 in) stems carrying flights in elegant array of purple, spurless flowers in spring.

Sempervivella *Crassulaceae*
S. alba (Plate 18, p. 78). A Himalayan making tufts of green, pink-flushed, fleshy leaves and producing short sprays of pure white flowers. Treat it like one of the sempervivums, which it resembles in general appearance.

Sempervivum *Crassulaceae*
It would be pointless outside the pages of a technical monograph to go into detail concerning the innumerable species and named hybrids and forms of this large and invaluable genus. They are all avid sun-lovers and, like the sedums, will endure very austere conditions whilst showing their appreciation of more generous treatment. Consult the pages of any alpine plant catalogue from which a selection can be made. All are desirable and offer a wide choice of rosettes of fleshy leaves. In most cases the flowers are of less importance than the extremely decorative foliage which is seen in a range of tints varying from green, and jade-green through purples to glowing red. The flowers on 20 cm (8 in) high stems are strange and magnificent, but the rosette from which they arise will die with them; younger rosettes around it then perpetuate the plant.

Serratula *Compositae*
S. seoanei. Usually grown under the erroneous name *S. shawii.* From S. Europe. Neat dwarf bushes of about 23 cm (9 in) with dark green, deeply cut leaves and branching stems carrying thistle-like heads of pink flowers. It blossoms in late summer and autumn.

Shortia *Diapensiaceae*
A small genus of lime-hating evergreen, dwarf plants, ideal occupants of a peat bed. Of the few species the Japanese *S. uniflora* is the one most likely to be available. Its woody stems carry rounded, firm leaves and large clear pink flowers with petals delicately fringed at the margins. It is likely to sulk for some time after being transplanted.

Sibthorpia *Scrophulariaceae*
S. europaea. From Europe, including Britain. It makes flat mats of creeping stems and is preferably grown in the forms whose tiny leaves are

variegated golden-green or silver. The flowers are inconspicuous. For a moist, cool position.

Silene *Caryophyllaceae*

S. acaulis. A typical alpine cushion plant with an immense distribution, extending from Britain throughout the Northern Hemisphere to Arctic America. Flat mats of tightly congested stems with tiny green leaves and, if you are fortunate, sheets of stemless pink flowers, but it is apt to be shy flowering in gardens. Give it full sun and austere conditions and hope for the best.

S. alpestris. From the Eastern Alps, easy and pretty, with 23 cm (9 in) branching stems and clouds of white flowers whose petals are daintily fringed.

S. hookeri. An American, and sufficiently temperamental to be accorded alpine-house treatment. Procumbent stems with narrow, hairy leaves and astonishingly large pink flowers, the petals cleft at their tips. Give it lime-free soil, gritty but with plenty of humus.

S. maritima. In the typical, single-flowered form this British native which dwells on our sea cliffs, is seldom cultivated, but it has a double-flowered form which is splendid when allowed to fall from a crevice or over the face of a wall. Grey leaves and large, fully double white flowers.

S. schafta. Showy, easy to grow and late flowering. The pink flowers are carried in profusion on 23 cm (9 in) stems from mid-summer until the autumn.

Sisyrinchium *Iridaceae*

The members of this large genus are natives of the American continent. Some of those with blue flowers, notably *S. angustifolium*, have entrenched themselves so firmly in our gardens as to become a nuisance, seeding themselves far and wide, but there are more virtuous members of the genus.

S. californicum. This, together with *S. convolutum*, forms tuffets of small, iris-like leaves and displays heads of bright yellow flowers.

S. douglasii. An aristocrat and a good perennial, although its appearances above ground are brief. In early spring it produces a few narrow leaves and 23 cm (9 in) stems from which swing bell-shaped flowers of wine-red. There is also a pretty albino. It will still be found in some catalogues as *S. grandiflorum*.

S. macounii. The species has blue flowers and is as yet seldom seen here, but the handsome albino form, *S. m.* 'Album' (Plate 19, p. 82) is a gem of gems. From its neat, dwarf tufts of narrow green leaves rise short stems bearing large, snow-white flowers.

Soldanella *Primulaceae*
A deservedly beloved race of European alpines which flower in the early
spring. They all like cool positions in gritty, humus-rich soil. They have
an undeserved reputation for being shy flowering. Their flower buds are
developed in the autumn, and rest close to the soil beneath the fleshy,
rounded leaves, invisible to the human eye, but not to the creeping slugs
which devour them with relish. There is a strong family resemblance
between the species and the several natural hybrids. They all carry, on
short, erect stems, clusters of pendent bells, the petals daintily fringed and
in shades of blue and purple. Amongst the best are S. *alpina*, S. *minima*, S.
montana and S. *villosa*. The last is probably the easiest of them all to grow.

Tanakaea *Saxifragaceae*
T. radicans. The only species in its genus and native to Japan. Numerous
rhizomes give forth many short stems clothed in evergreen, leathery
leaves toothed at the margins. The clusters of small white flowers are seen
in spring and early summer. For lime-free soil and a cool position.

Thalictrum *Ranunculaceae*
Commonly, and rightly, regarded as tall border plants, there are several
dwarf species useful for summer flowering in the rock garden. One of the
best and the one most likely to be available, is *T. kiusianum*, a neat little
23 cm (9 in) dwarf from Japan whose wiry stems carry loose and elegant
heads of purple flowers over the dainty, fern-like foliage. It is hardy but is
good enough to deserve alpine house treatment.

Thlaspi *Cruciferae*
Those who have been fortunate enough to tread the high places of the
European Alps will have encountered and fallen in love with *T. rotundifolium*. It grows in the high screes and is somewhat reluctant to accept
captivity, but give it almost pure grit in a sunny place or in the alpine
house and you may hope to enjoy its neat heads of fragrant rose-lavender
flowers set over tufts of fleshy, dark green leaves.

Thymus *Labiatae*
A genus not to be ignored and varying from the flat mats of the many
forms of *T. serpyllum* to those of more shrubby habit. They are all sun-
lovers and easily grown in any good soil.
    T. × citriodorus. This is the lemon-scented thyme, usually grown in
the forms 'Silver Queen', silver variegated, and 'Aureus', also variegated,
but in shades of yellow and gold. Neat 23 cm (9 in) bushes.
    T. 'Doone Valley'. A hybrid of uncertain parentage, but a delightful

Plate 19. *Sisyrinchium macounii* 'Album'. This handsome albino form has neat, dwarf tufts of narrow green leaves, with snow-white flowers on short stems.

mounded cushion of olive-green leaves freckled with gold. The crimson buds open into lavender flowers.

    T. herba-barona. Entangled woody stems and dark-green leaves, the whole plant strongly caraway-scented. The flowers are purple, in small, rounded heads.

    T. serpyllum. The well-loved common creeping, wild thyme which exists in several cultivated forms with flowers which may be white, pink

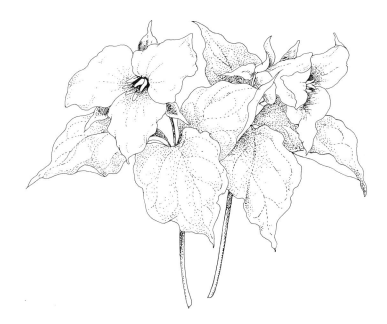

Fig. 15 *Trillium grandiflorum*

or rich crimson-red according to kind. Invaluable for carpeting the
ground in sunny places or as fillers for crannies between paving stones.
The foliage is almost as variable as the flowers and may be dark green or
grey or golden-variegated. The plants in cultivation are correctly termed
T. praecox articus (T. drucei).

Tiarella *Saxifragaceae*
T. cordifolia. The pretty foam flower from N. America is a good inhabi-
tant of cool, north-facing or shady places. It makes low mats of softly
hairy, bronze-tinted leaves over which hover the many spires of cream-
white flowers during spring and early summer.

Trifolium *Leguminosae*
T. alpinum. From the Alps of Europe. From its deep-delving roots spring
leaves composed of three narrow leaflets. The heads of pink and purple
clover flowers are borne on 10cm (4in) stems.

Trillium *Liliaceae*
The most frequently encountered, and one of the easiest and best of the

Fig. 16 *Verbascum* × 'Letitia'

numerous species is *T. grandiflorum* (Fig. 15). It prefers a place where the soil is moisture retentive and will grow fully in the open or in light shade. A herald of spring, it develops from its deeply-delving fleshy roots clumps of broad, three-parted leaves and carries on bold, erect stems large, snow-white flowers which subsequently adopt a tinge of pink as they age.

Trollius *Ranunculaceae*
The globe flowers are usually regarded as tall plants for bog gardens or moist positions, but *T. acaulis* from the Himalaya is the pygmy of the race. It likes a place where the soil does not dry out rapidly and there it makes tiny tufts of divided leaves and carries on stems no more than 10 cm (4 in) high, rounded, golden-yellow flowers. Only a trifle taller is *T. pumilus*, from north India and China. Its leaves are five-parted and the rounded golden flowers are carried on stems only slightly taller than those of *T. acaulis*.

Tunica *Caryophyllaceae*
T. saxifraga. Not an aristocrat, but a useful, easy and decorative small, summer-flowering plant for a sunny position. Showers of pink flowers on short stems and there is a form named 'Rosette' which has fully double blossoms.

Vancouveria *Berberidaceae*
V. hexandra. A graceful plant for a cool situation. Leaves divided into leaflets, on wiry stems and sprays of white flowers on 23 cm (9 in) stems in spring.

Verbascum *Scrophulariaceae*
Most of the members of this genus are border plants, but there is at least one admirable rock garden hybrid in the form of *V.* × 'Letitia', which makes a mounded, rounded bushlet smothered for weeks on end in summer with yellow 'mullein' flowers (Fig. 16). Height approximately 23 cm (9 in); spread approximately 30 cm (12 in). For a dry and sunny place.

Veronica *Scrophulariaceae*
A considerable number of the plants hitherto known as veronicas have now been placed in other genera, notably *Hebe*. The few listed below are all desirable rock garden or alpine house plants. They are sun-lovers and present no problems unless specified in their descriptions.
V. bombycina. For the alpine house. It comes from the Lebanon and makes prostrate mats of tiny, silver leaves studded with china-blue flowers.
V. filiformis. A warning must always accompany this pretty but invasive plant. It will spread far and wide but, in a safe position, will prove delightful when its mats are sheeted with soft blue flowers. Good ground cover, even in light shade.
V. gentianoides. Perhaps a trifle tall, but elegant when carrying the blue flowers on 38 cm (15 in) stems. There is a desirable form with silver variegated foliage.
V. pectinata. Low tufts of trailing stems and grey, softly hairy leaves adorned with short spikes of blue/pink flowers.
V. prostrata. This dwarf exists in a number of named forms, such as 'Spode Blue', 'Royal Blue', 'Alba' (white), 'Mrs. Holt' (pink), 'Silver Queen' (silvery-blue) and 'Nana', which is very dwarf and blue flowered.
V. telephifolia. Another for the alpine house. Creeping stems and waxy grey leaves. The flowers are clear china-blue. Gritty soil and water with care.

Plate 20. *Viola cornuta* is a charming flower, both in its shape and in the generosity and duration of its flowering. There are sky-blue, blue-purple and white forms.

Viola *Violaceae*

V. aetolica (saxatilis). The neatest of neat tufts with toothed leaves and clear yellow flowers. Occasionally the two upper petals may be violet.

V. biflora. This dainty species peeps out at you from rock crevices in the Alps. Kidney-shaped leaves and twin flowers of clear yellow. It likes a cool-position and gritty soil.

V. cornuta. An invaluable and long-flowering species (Plate 20, p. 86). Typically the flowers are rich purple, but there is a delightful albino which breeds true from seed.

V. cucullata. A N. American for a cool position. Mats of scaly rhizomes and broad, toothed leaves. The flowers are usually white, the petals veined with violet lines.

V. elatior. Almost a shrub with erect, 30 cm (12 in) high stems and showers of soft lavender flowers.

V. verecunda yakushimana. The smallest of all violets, from Japan. Minute tufts of wee leaves and miniature flowers of white with purple veins on the tiny petals. Ideal for stone trough and sink gardens.

Waldsteinia *Rosaceae*

W. ternata (trifolia). An easy, long-flowering, mat-forming evergreen sheeted throughout the summer with sprays of golden flowers.

Weldenia *Commelinaceae*

W. candida. This is a beautiful rarity from the craters of extinct volcanoes in Mexico and Guatemala. The only species in its genus it is eagerly sought and carefully tended by those who like to have in their gardens a few of the rare gems of the alpine world, and this is one that is best grown in deep pots or pans and treasured in an alpine house or unheated greenhouse.

It has deeply-delving, almost tuberous roots from which rise annually tufts of thick, broad and pointed dark green leaves. From the centre of the rosette rise clusters of dazzlingly white, cup shaped flowers – indeed, it is the whitest flower that I know. The Guatemalan form differs only from the Mexican one in having curious tufts of white hairs on the leaf surfaces.

Zauschneria *Onagraceae*

Z. californica. Magnificent in late summer and autumn, in a hot and dry position when it covers itself with sprays of scarlet tubular flowers. The most desirable form is named 'Splendens'.

CHAPTER 4

PLANTS FOR SPECIAL POSITIONS AND CONDITIONS

PLANTS FOR SPECIAL POSITIONS AND CONDITIONS

Some of the plants listed in the following categories of plants suited to various positions and conditions are not described in the body of this book, but they are all readily available from commercial sources.

PLANTS SPECIALLY SUITABLE FOR HOT, DRY POSITIONS IN FULL SUN

Acaenas
Alyssums
Cistuses
Cytisuses
Dorycnium hirsutum
Genistas
Halimiums
Helianthemums
Helichrysums

Hypericums
Linums
Lithophragma
Raoulias
Santolinas
Sedums
Sempervivums
Zauschnerias

PLANTS WHICH WILL FLOURISH IN POOR SOIL AND UNDER ADVERSE CONDITIONS

Acaenas
Ajugas
Allium moly
Antennarias
Anthemises
Armerias

Borago laxiflora
Campanula poscharskyana
Cerastium tomentosum
Cotulas
Epimediums
Festucas

Geranium sanguineum forms
Gypsophilas
Helianthemums
Hieraceums
Pachysandras
Polygonum vaccinifolium
Potentilla megalantha

Sagina glabra 'Aurea'
Saponaria ocymoides
Sedums
Sempervivums
Thymus serpyllum forms
Veronica filiformis
Vincas

PLANTS FOR MOIST POSITIONS OR COOL SHADE

Achlys triphylla
Anemone nemorosa forms
Astilbes
Cassiopes
Cyclamen species
Dicentras
Gentiana (autumn flowering)
Geranium phaeum
Geranium sylvaticum
Hostas (small forms)
Houstonia

Linnaea
Lysimachia nummularia 'Aurea'
Maianthemum bifolium
Meconopses
Mentha requienii
Mimulus, all forms
Nepeta hederacea 'Variegata'
Primulus (bog and candelabra)
Ranunculus ficaria forms
Tiarellas
Trilliums

PLANTS FOR DRY SHADE

Ajugas
Campanula portenschlagiana
Chiastophyllum oppositifolium
Convallarias
Geranium hybrids
Geranium endressii
Geranium phaeum

Geranium sylvaticum
Lamium maculatum varieties
Pachysandras
Polygonatum
Polygonum tenuicaule
Saxifraga umbrosa forms
Vincas

PLANTS FOR FREE-STANDING OR
RETAINING WALLS

Achilleas (dwarf kinds)
Aethionemas
Alchemilla mollis
Alyssums

Dryas octopetala
Erinuses
Erodiums
Genistas

Androsace lanuginosa
  'Leichtlinii'
Androsace primuloides varieties
Anthemis cupaniana
Arabis albida forms
Arenarias
Armerias
Aspleniums
Aubrietas
Campanulas
Chiastophyllum oppositifolium
Cotoneaster 'Teulon Porter'
Dianthuses

Gypsophilas
Heliathemums
Hypericum olympicum
Iberises
Lewisias
Phlox douglasii forms
Phlox subulata forms
Polygonum vaccinifolium
Ramondas
Saxifraga aizoon forms
Sedums
Veronica prostrata forms
Zauschnerias

PLANTS FOR GROUND-COVERING AND FOR
PLANTING BETWEEN PAVING STONES

Those especially suitable for paving are marked (P)

Acaenas (P)
Achilleas dwarf (P)
Ajugas
Antennarias (P)
Anthemis 'Treneague'
Arenaria balearica
Armerias (P)
Bolax glebaria (P)
Campanula cochlearifolia (P)
Campanula poscharskyana
Cotoneaster 'Skogholm'
Cotulas (P)
Crassula sedifolia (P)
Dianthus arvernensis 'Alba' (P)
Euphorbia robbiae
Festucas
Genista pilosa
Geranium collinum

Geranium sanguineum
  'Lancastriense'
Goodenia repens (P)
Haplocarpha ruepellii
Herniaria glabra (P)
Hypsella longiflora (P)
Lamium maculatum forms
Lippia canescens (P)
Lotus corniculatus 'Flore Plena'
Luzuriaga radicans
Mazus reptans (P)
Mentha requienii (P)
Pachysandras
Raoulias (P)
Ruscus aculeatus
Sagina glabra 'Aurea' (P)
Saxifraga aizoon forms
Thymus serpyllum forms (P)
Veronica filiformis

PLANTS FOR STONE TROUGHS AND SINK GARDENS

Acorus gramineas 'Pusillus'
Aethionema 'Warley Rose'
Androsace sempervivoides
Antennarias
Arenaria tetraquetra 'Granatensis'
Armeria caespitosa
Berberis irwinii 'Coralina Compacta'
Bolax glebaria
Campanula arvatica
Campanula cochlearifolia
Campanula excisa
Centaurium scilloides
Crassula sedifolia
Dianthus alpinus
Dianthus arvernensis
Dianthus erinaceus
Dianthus lemsii
Dianthus musalae
Draba rigida
Dryas octopetala 'Minor'
Erigeron aureus
Erigeron trifidus
Erinuses

Erodium reichardii 'Roseum'
Genista pilosa 'Procumbens'
Gentiana verna 'Angulosa'
Geranium × 'Ballerina'
Geranium dalmaticum
Geranium pylzowianum
Geranium subcaulescens
Globularia bellidifolia
Gypsophila dubia
Gypsophila fratensis
Hebe bidwillii
Hebe buchananii 'Minor'
Helianthemum 'Amy Baring'
Helichrysum frigidum
Helichrysum milfordiae
Hypsella longiflora
Iris cristata
Lewisias
Mentha requeinii
Micromeria corsica
Morisia monanthos
Oxalis enneaphylla
Primula bilecki
Primula marginata
Ranunculus montanus 'Molten Gold'

PLANTS FOR AUTUMN, WINTER AND SPRING FLOWERING

Adonis amurensis
Cyclamen coum
Cyclamen hederifolium
Cyclamen purpurascens
Cyclamen repandum

Eranthis hyemalis
Galanthus – most kinds
Gentiana sino-ornata
Hepatica nobilis
Saxifraga fortunei

PLANTS FOR THE ALPINE HOUSE

Aethionema 'Warley Rose'
Anacyclus depressus
Androsace, all kinds
Arabis bryoides
Arenaria tetraquetra
Asperula suberosa
Calceolaria darwinii
Crassula sarcocaulis
Cyclamen, all kinds
Dionysia aretioides
Erigeron aureus
Gypsophila aretioides

Hebe buchananii 'Minor'
Lewisias, all kinds
Omphalodes luciliae
Pleiones, all kinds
Ramonda myconii
Salix boydii
Ramonda myconii
Salix boydii
Saxifraga, all the 'Kabschia' kinds
Saxifraga grisebachii
Sedum humifusum

INDEX

Acaena adscendens, 17
  buchananii, 17
  glabra, 17
  microphylla, 17
  novae-zealandiae, 17 '
  sanguisorbae, 17
Acantholimon, 18–19
  glumaceum, 18
  venustem, 18
Aceriphyllum rossii, 19
Achillea ageratifolia, 19
  × argentea, 19
  aurea, 19
  clavenae, 19
  grisebachii, 19
  moschata, 20
  nana, 20
  tomentosa, 20
  umbellata, 20
  × wilczekii, 20
Acorus gramineus, 20
Adenophora confusa, 21
  lamarckii, 21
  nikoensis, 21
  sinensis, 21
  takedai, 21
  tashiroi, 21
Aethionema armenum, 21
  coridifolium, 21
  grandiflorum, 21
  pulchellum, 21
  theodorum, 21
Ajuga reptans, 22
Alchemilla alpina, 22
Allium amabile, 22
  beesianum, 22
  caeruleum, 22
  cyaneum, 22
  flavum, 23
  karataviense, 23
  moly, 23
  narcissiflorum, 23
  triquetrum, 23
Alpine house, 10–12
Alpine plants (general)
  compost, 7, 8, 9
  definition, 7
  drainage, 7
  for alpine house, 92
  for autumn/winter/
    spring flowering, 91
  for dry shade, 89
  for ground-cover, 90
  for hot dry position,
    88
  for moist position, 89

for paving stones, 90
for poor soil, 88–89
for stone troughs, 91
for walls, 89–90
needs, 7–8
planting season, 8
Alyssum saxatile, 23–24
Anacyclus depressus, 24
Anagallis linifolia, 24
  tenella, 24
Anchusa caespitosa, 24
Androsace alpina, 25
  carnea, 25
  chamaejasme, 25
  ciliata, 25
  cylindrica, 25
  hedraeantha, 25
  helvetica, 25
  hirtella, 25
  lanuginosa, 25–26
  primuloides, 26
  pubescens, 26
  pyrenaica, 26
  sempervivoides, 26
  vandellii, 26
  villosa, 26
  watkinsii, 26
  yunnanensis, 26
Andryala aghardii, 26
Anemone apennina, 27
  blanda, 27
  magellanica, 27
  nemorosa, 27
  ranunculoides, 27
  sylvestris, 28
Antennaria dioica, 28
Anthemis biebersteinii, 29
  cupaniana, 29
  nobilis, 29
Anthericum liliago, 31
  ramosum, 31
Anthyllis vulneraria, 31
Antirrhinum asarina,
  see Asarina
Aphyllanthes
  monspeliensis, 31
Aquilegia alpina, 31
  bertolonii, 31
  caerulea, 31
  discolor, 31
  ecalcarata,
    see Semiaquilegia
  flabellata, 31–32
  jonesii, 32
  viridiflora, 32
Arabis androsacea, 32

  bryoides, 32
  caucasica, 32
  ferdinandii-coburgii, 32
Arcterica, 32
Arenaria balearica, 33
  bertolonii, 33
  ledebouriana, 33
  montana, 33
  purpurascens, 33
  tetraquetra, 33
Arisaema
  candidissimum, 33
Arisarum proboscideum, 33
Armeria caespitosa, 33
  maritima, 33–34
Arnica montana, 34
Artemisia asoana, 34
  glacialis, 34
  lanata, 35
  schmidtiana, 35
  stelleriana, 35
Asarina procumbens, 35
Asperula gussonii, 35
  hirta, 35
  suberosa, 36
Aster alpinus, 36
  bellidiastrum,
    see Bellidiastrum
  natalensis, 36
Aubrieta, 14

Bellidiastrum michelii, 36
Bellis rotundifolia, 36
  sylvestris, 36
Berberis empetrifolia, 36

Calamintha alpina, 37
  grandiflora, 37
Colceolaria darwinii, 37
  tenella, 37
Campanula allionii, 38
  arvatica, 38
  betulaefolia, 38–40
  carpatica, 40
  cochleariifolia, 40
  formaneckiana, 40
  garganica, 40
  'G, F. Wilson', 40
  linifolia, 40
  morettiana, 40–41
  muralis, see
    C. portenschlagiana
  portenschlagiana, 41
  poscharskyana, 41
  thyrsoides, 41
Cassiope, 41–42

lycopodioides, 42
Cheiranthus cheiri, 42
Chrysanthemum hosmariense,
   see *Leucanthemum*
Cistus, 88
Compost, 7, 8, 9
Convolvulus boissieri, 42
Cuttings, 14–16
Cyananthus lobatus, 42
Cyclamen coum, 42
   hederifolium, 42
   neapolitanum, see
     C. hederifolium
   purpurascens, 42
   repandum, 42
Cytisus, 88

Daphne blagayana, 44
   cneorum, 44
   collina, 44
   petraea, 44
Dianthus, 44
   alpinus, 44
   arvernensis, 44
   deltoides, 44
   gratianopolitanus, 44
   knappii, 44
   superbus, 45
Dionysia aretioides, 45
Division, 16
Draba aizoides, 45
   bryoides, 45
   dedeana, 45
   mollissima, 45
Drainage, 7
Dryas octopetala, 45

Edraianthus, 47
Erigeron aurantiacus, 47
   aureus, 47
   flettii, 47
   karvinskianus, 48
   mucronatus, see
     E. karvinskianus
Erinus alpinus, 48
Erodium chrysanthum, 48
   corsicum, 48
   reichardii, 48
Euryops acraeus, 48

Frankenia laevis, 48
   thymifolia, 48

Gentiana, 13
   acaulis, 49
   asclepiadea, 49

bavarica, 49
bellidifolia, 49
brachyphylla, 49
farreri, 49
imbricata, 49
× 'Inverleith', 49
lagodechiana, 49
lutea, 49
pneumonanthe, 49
saxosa, 49
sino-ornata, 49
verna, 51
Geranium argenteum, 51
   cinereum, 51
   dalmaticum, 51
   farreri, 51
   renardii, 51
   sanguineum, 51
   wallichianum, 51
Geum montanum, 51
   reptans, 51
Globularia, 51
Gypsophila repens, 51–52

Haberlea rhodopensis, 52
Helianthemum, 14
   nummularium, 52–53
Helichrysum bellidioides, 53
   frigidum, 53
   milfordiae, 53
Hepatica, 34
   nobilis, 53
   transsilvanica, 53
   triloba, see *H. nobilis*
Houstonia caerulea, 54
Hutchinsia alpina, 54
Hypericum coris, 54
   empetrifolium, 54
   olympicum, 54
   reptans, 54
   trichocaulon, 54

Iberis sempervivens, 54
Iris chamaeris, 54–56
   cristata, 56
   gracilipes, 56
   innominata, 56
   lacustris, 56
   pumila, 56
   unguicularis, 56

Jasione jankae, 56

Kalmiopsis leachiana, 56

Leontopodium alpinum, 56

Leucanthemum hosmariense,
   56
Lewisia, 13
   brachycalyx, 57
   × 'Pinkie', 57
   rediviva, 57
   tweedyi, 57
Lilium, 14
Linaria alpina, 57
Linnaea borealis, 57
Linum campanulatum, 57
   capitatum, 57
   flavum, 57
   monogynum, 58
   narbonense, 58
Lithophragma diffusum, 58
Lotus corniculatus, 58
Lychnis alpina, 59

Maianthemum bifolium, 59
Mazus pumilio, 59
   radicans, 59
   reptans, 59
Meconopsis
   quintuplinervia, 59
Mentha requienii, 60
Mibora minima, 60
Mimulus cupreus, 60
   primuloides, 60
Minuartia verna, 60
Moltkaea petraea, 60
Morisia monanthos, 60
Mukdenia rossii, 19

Nierembergia repens, 60

Oenothera acaulis, 61
   caespitosa, 61
   missouriensis, 61
Omphalodes
   cappadocica, 61
   luciliae, 61
   verna, 61
Onosma taurica, 61
Origanum dictamnus, 61
   rotundifolium, 62
Oxalis adenophylla, 62
   enneaphylla, 62
   lobata, 62

Papaver alpinum, 62
Paradisea liliastrum, 62
Parnassia palustris, 62
Peat-beds, 10
Penstemon, 62–64
Petrocallis pyrenaica, 64

Phlox, 14
    adsurgens, 64
    amoena, 64
    'Chattahoochee', 64
    douglasii, 64
    subulata, 64
    Physoplexis comosa, 64
Pieris nana, 32
Pinguicula grandiflora, 65
Pleione formosana, 65
    limprichtii, 65
    pricei, 65
Polygala chamaebuxus, 65
Polygonum vaccinifolium, 65
Potentilla alba, 66
    aurea, 66
    megalantha, 66
    nitida, 66
    × *tonguei*, 66
Primula, 13
    allionii, 66
    auricula, 68
    farinosa, 68
    frondosa, 68
    hirsuta, 68
    juliae, 68
    × *juliana*, 68
    latifolia, 68
    marginata, 68
    minima, 68
    × *pubescens*, 68
    vulgaris, 68
Propagation, 13–16
Ptilotrichum spinosum, 68–69
Pulsatilla, 13, 27
    vulgaris, 69

Ramonda pyrenaica, 69
Ranunculus, 13
    alpestris, 69
    amplexicaulis, 69
    calandrinioides, 69
    ficaria, 69
    montanus, 69
Raoulia australis, 71
    glabra, 71
    hookeri, 71
    lutescens, 71
Repotting, 12
Rhodohypoxis baurii, 71
Rubus arcticus, 71

Sagina glabra, 72
Salix, 72
    boydii, 72
Salvia argentea, 72
Samolus repens, 73
Sanguinaria canadensis, 73
Saponaria ocymoides, 73
Saxifraga, 73
    aizoides, 73
    aizoon, 73
    × *apiculata*, 74
    'Bob Hawkins', 74
    'Boston Spa', 74
    burseriana, 74
    caesia, 74
    callosa, 75
    cochlearis, 75
    cotyledon, 75
    cuscutiformis, 75
    'Esther', 75
    fortunei, 75
    granulata, 75
    grisebachii, 75
    irvingii, 75
    'Kathleen Pinsent', 75
    latepetiolata, 75
    lilacina, 75
    longifolia, 75
    oppositifolia, 76
    retusa, 76
    'Tumbling Waters', 75–76
    umbrosa, 76
    × *urbium*, 76
Scabiosa columbaria, 77
Scleranthus biflorus, 77
    uniflorus, 77
Scutellaria scordiifolia, 77
Sedum album, 77
    caeruleum, 77
    cauticolum, 77
    humifusum, 77
    lydium, 77
    oreganum, 78
    primuloides, 78
    pulchellum, 78
    spathulifolium, 78
Seed raising, 13–14
Semiaquilegia adoxioides, 79
Sempervivella alba, 79
Sempervivum, 79
Serratula soanei, 79

Shortia uniflora, 79
Sibthorpia europaea, 79–80
Silene acaulis, 80
    alpestris, 80
    hookeri, 80
    maritima, 80
    schafta, 80
Sisyrinchium
    angustifolium, 80
    californicum, 80
    douglasii, 80
    macounii, 80
Soldanella, 81

Tanakaea radicans, 81
Thalictrum kiusianum, 81
Thlaspi rotundifolium, 81
Thymus × *citriodorus*, 81
    'Doone Valley', 82
    herba-barona, 82
    serpyllum, 82
Tiarella cordifolia, 83
Trifolium alpinum, 83
Trillium grandiflorum, 84
Trollius acaulis, 84
    pumilus, 84
Tunica saxifraga, 85

Vancouveria hexandra, 85
Ventilation, 11–12, 15
Verbascum × 'Letitia', 85
Veronica bombycina, 85
    filiformis, 85
    gentianoides, 85
    pectinata, 85
    prostrata, 85
    telephifolia, 85
Viola aetolica, 87
    biflora, 87
    cornuta, 87
    cucullata, 87
    elatior, 87
    verecunda
    yakushimana, 87

Waldsteinia ternata, 87
Walls, 10
Watering, 8, 9, 10, 12, 15
Weldenia candida, 87

Zauschneria californica, 87